BASICS OF ...
POTTERY

"*He wrought a work upon the wheels, and the vessel that he made of clay was marred in the hands of the Potter: so he made it again another vessel, as seemed good to the Potter to make it.*"
—Jeremiah

BASICS OF ...
POTTERY

GEORGE J. COX, ARCA
TEACHERS COLLEGE
COLUMBIA UNIVERSITY

Basics of ...
is an imprint of
ABSOLUTELY AMAZING eBOOKS

Published by Whiz Bang LLC, 926 Truman Avenue, Key West, Florida 33040, USA.

Basics of ... Pottery copyright © 2014 by Gee Whiz Entertainment LLC. Electronic compilation/ paperback edition copyright © 2014 by Whiz Bang LLC. The first edition of this book was published by The Macmillan Company in 1914.

All rights reserved. No part of this book may be reproduced, scanned, or transmitted in any form or by any means, electronic or mechanical, including photocopying, recording, or any information storage and retrieval system, without permission in writing from the publisher. Please do not participate in or encourage piracy of copyrighted materials in violation of the authors' rights. Purchase only authorized ebook editions.

While the authors have made every effort to provide accurate information, neither the publisher nor the authors assume any responsibility for errors, or for changes that occur after publication. Further, the publisher does not have any control over and does not assume any responsibility for author or third-party websites or their contents. How the ebook displays on a given reader is beyond the publisher's control.

Statement by Archivist: *Much of the material in this book is in the public domain because it was published in the United States before 1923.*

For information contact:
Publisher@AbsolutelyAmazingEbooks.com

ISBN-13: 978-0692344224 (Basics of ...)
ISBN-10: 0692344225

"O Master, pardon me, if yet in vain
Thou art my Master, and I fail to bring
Before men's eyes the image of the thing
My heart is filled with."
—William Morris

EXPLANATION

In such a spacious craft as Pottery it is difficult to steer a fair course between the empirical and the scientific. With that in mind this book sets out to tell in simple terms some of the processes of Potting, practicable to the student and to the more finished craftsman.

It is an intricate task to combine successfully the viewpoints of the artist and the scientist; but it seems that, without neglecting the many benefits bestowed by the advance of science, the Potter should stand with the former. The best in his craft has been produced by men that were artists rather than chemists. And what has been accomplished by loving, patient craftsmanship may surely be done again only in such ways.

To the artist craftsman, for whom chiefly this book is intended, a little scientific knowledge is a dangerous thing; for that reason no great stress is laid on formulas and analysis. Unless thoroughly understood they are a hindrance rather than an aid.

Although many schools teach elementary pottery, the expense of equipment possibly delays its introduction on a larger scale. For that reason I have preferred to err on the side of over-exactness of description and profuseness of illustration.

The slight historical review and introductory remarks are to be excused on the ground that they are intended to help to a study of the best work of the best periods, and so to foster a taste for the finest Ceramics. This is a vital matter when laying the foundations of a craft so fascinating and so full of alluring avenues to beckon the student from the true path.

To the scientific critic I would offer a hundred books with a thousand different compounds; amongst none of them will he find how to make a Sung bowl or a Rakka drug pot.

This book will achieve its purpose if it sets one or two sincere students to the making of some of the many beautiful objects of utility and art with which the craft abounds. Then it will have done something, if never so little, to accelerate the arrival of that time when the artist will come once more into his own in the most ancient and noble of Crafts.

Some of the many books consulted, to which I am indebted, are given at the end of the book. Among friends my thanks are especially due to Richard Lunn, Esq., of the Royal College of Art, London, and to Professor Arthur Wesley Dow of Teachers College, Columbia University, for my introduction to and opportunity of further study of the Craft to which I subscribe myself an humble devotee.

- G. J. C.

TABLE OF CONTENTS

CHAPTER

I.	Historical Summary
II.	Clays and Pastes
III.	Built Shapes
IV.	Molding, Casting, and Pressing
V.	Jigger and Jolley Work
VI.	Thrown Shapes
VII.	Turning Or Shaving
VIII.	Tile-Making
IX.	Drying: Finishing
X.	Firing Biscuit
XI.	Glost Firing
XII.	Glazes and Lusters
XIII.	Decoration
XIV.	Figurines
XV.	Kilns
XVI.	The Educational Value of Pottery
APPENDIX	Equipment for a Small Pottery or a School
APPENDIX	Glossary and General Information

BASICS OF ...
POTTERY

CHAPTER I
Historical Summary

"After this he led them into his garden, where was great variety of Flowers. Then said he again, Behold, the Flowers are diverse in stature, in quality, and color, and smell, and virtue, and some are better than some."

—Bunyan

Without attempting a history of pottery which, however brief, would be somewhat out of place in a Craft Book, a short summary of its evolution, emphasizing those periods in which it was most beautifully developed, seems essential to help the beginner in the selection and appreciation of good form, color, and decoration. These are very vital matters and easily overlooked in the struggle to acquire a craft that is full of fascination from the first fumbled shape upon the wheel to the finished product of time and art and craft.

Too much stress cannot be laid upon the importance of close study of the best work, both ancient and modern; for it is a truism that however handily a craftsman may work, his output will be worthless if he has not, with his increasing powers of technique, developed a sound judgment and refined taste. Today, these alone can replace the lost traditions of the old masters.

The Potter's Craft had a coeval birth in various parts of the earth, but the obscurity is such that no clear idea can be gained of its antiquity. It was, probably, the first form of handicraft, if we except the fashioning of flints and clubs. Accident or the funeral pyre may have suggested the extraordinary durability the clay shape obtained when burned, and doubtless siliceous glazes were first the result of chance. All early work was built up by hand and for that reason possesses wide mouths and simple forms. The introduction of the wheel is lost in a mist of time, but drawings from the tombs of Beni Hassan show the potter at his wheel substantially as he works in Asia to this day. The wheel-made or thrown shape is distinguished by far more grace and symmetry than the built shape, and by an infinitely greater variety of form.

In burial mounds from prehistoric Egypt are found many bowls and platters rudely scratched, and the earliest examples from mounds, lake dwellings, and tombs show the quick development of the pot, not only as an object of utility, but as a vehicle of art.

The first kinds of decoration were incised lines followed by strappings and bandings, painted stripes and scrolls and hieroglyphs, with later additions in slip and modeled clay. Primitive wares from their method of production exhibit an interesting similarity of shape and style in such widely divergent countries as China, Egypt, and Peru.

It was only when the craftsman had acquired considerable dexterity that we find his nationality influencing his shapes and producing the wonderful variety in form and decoration that characterizes and distinguishes the pottery of all nations. Once established, the prevalence of type is strong. This traditional style is particularly noticeable in Egypt, much modern work being identical with that of the early dynasties.

George J. Cox

Before turning to more sophisticated work it would be well to learn the lesson of simplicity and fitness here taught by primitive folks. The simple beginning leads to the simple, strong, and satisfying end. Much of this primitive work is inspiring for its freshness or naïveté; its unspoiled innate taste allied to downright common sense. Properly approached, it should be a sure corrective to any desire for unsightly *new* shapes or extravagance in decoration. A few careful studies will do much to drive home this valuable lesson in fine, simple line and spacing.

In Egypt the thrown shape was not distinguished by any extraordinary beauty or variety. Nevertheless their small *Ushabti*, glazed gods and demons, show a very advanced knowledge of colored enamels, and their fabrication of a hard sandy paste for glazing shows the first great step in the science of pottery. Their glaze was purely alkaline.

The Assyrians appear to have been the first to use colored tin glazes, and although few pieces of pottery survive, the enameled friezes from Korsobad and Sousa are striking evidence of their proficiency in tile-making.

From Egypt and Mesopotamia the craft spread east and west to Phœnicia, Attica, and Greece; through Persia and Arabia to India. Here it mingled with currents from China, then invading Korea, Japan, and Siam, the united floods rising until the potter was a power in every land.

Phœnician pottery forms, with Cretan and early Grecian, a beautiful sequence from the primitive work of early dynasties to the refinements of later Grecian wares.

It will prove an interesting and instructive study to trace the developments that led finally to the zenith of Greek pottery. The primitive Hissarlik ware leads through

Mycenaean, Dipylon, Phalæron, Rhodian, and Corinthian right up to the wonderful figure vases of about 300 B.C. Although limited in paste and color, with a thin transparent glaze or luster, these vases were exquisitely fashioned. Large and small shapes of wide diversity were decorated in black, red, and white, ornament and figures both drawn straight on to the body with a sureness of touch and refinement of line that excite the envy of a master. Many of their forms are strongly influenced by contemporary bronze work and for that reason are not the best guides for shapes. Their incomparable terra-cottas known as Tanagras form a link between Pottery and Sculpture.

Again, from Phœnician work one may see dimly by way of Samian, Rhodian and old Cairene wares the lineage of the royal wares of Persia, and recent investigations point to Old Cairo as the birthplace of luster.

From Persia come some of the finest pottery, painted in colors and lusters, that the world can show. Their wares stand pre-eminent in that class wherein the chief beauty is the painted decoration. Their one-color pieces, whilst not comparable with the Chinese, nevertheless reach a high standard. Their lusters have never been surpassed or rarely equaled. Their shapes are true potter's shapes, and a delight to the eye. The finest pieces were painted in simple blues, greens, reds, and faint purples, with black penciling. This appears to have been done on an engobe of finely ground flint, and covered with an alkaline glaze giving a broken white ground.

This would account in some measure for the extraordinary freshness of both drawing and color. Later on raised ornament, finely conceived and used with restraint, is seen along with pierced decoration having translucent effects.

Rhodes and Damascus produced a somewhat coarser ware, but bold and free in brushwork and varied with a bright red. Syrian pottery abounds in virile individual shapes. Turkey also was not without a fine and vigorous style.

Much time can be most profitably spent studying the masterpieces of Persia. A representative collection like that at South Kensington will show vases, bottles, bowls, pots, and tiles in bewildering variety and of infinite freshness. They are directly painted, with free renderings of flowers within geometric forms and often with an inscription in rich Arabic characters. The exquisite Moore Collection in the Metropolitan Museum, New York City, is smaller but is remarkable for the unusually high standard of taste shown in its acquisition. At its purest period human or animal figures were rarely or never represented and those shapes or tiles with such decoration belong to a more decadent but still fine period.

Again we have the eternal lesson of simplicity and fitness. Again it will be borne in upon the student that originality does not mean weirdness, but rather a fresh spontaneous treatment of simple, well-known natural forms, with, above all, a fine appreciation of good line and space. No sincere student can fail to develop here a respect and veneration of a craft and of craftsmen capable of producing such glorious works.

From this teeming home the craft spread to Arabia and west across the Mediterranean to Spain. Here in the Twelfth Century the Moors were producing their famous Hispano-

Mooresque lustered wares. Their large plaques offer a wonderful variety of pure brushwork ornament with spirited heraldic additions. Sometimes the backs of these dishes are as beautifully lustered as the fronts.

For a proper appreciation of their purely geometric decoration and its possibilities in pottery we must turn to the Alcazar at Madrid. Here the use of opaque tin glaze permitted the extensive use of a coarse body for tiles and bricks. The Moors, however, first introduced glazes with a lead base and from that time we begin to lose the fresh *wet* color always associated with the alkaline glazes of the Persians. Analysis shows that they used lead, but only occasionally and in small quantities, to aid their lusters. The lustered wares of Spain declined late in the Thirteenth Century, but not before its exportation to Italy by way of Majorca had stimulated the production of Italian Majolica. Della Robbia, about 1415, succeeded in coloring his tin glazes, and his finely modeled but somewhat crudely colored reliefs usher in the era of Italian Faience. Patronized by the nobles the craft quickly took root and was blossoming profusely at Urbino, Gubbio, Pesaro, Faenza and other cities at the end of the Fifteenth Century.

Here we break ground and leave the chaste simplicity of the golden age to riot a blaze of exuberant decoration. Scraffito, slip, inlaid, applied, incised, raised, embossed and modeled and painted embellishments; all are here. This era is chiefly notable for its splendid ruby lusters and the remarkable power and freedom, amounting to absolute abandon, of the brushwork and drawing shown by its artists. They used their lusters to heighten the effects of their painting and the results are in keeping with that romantic age. Alongside of it our best modern work is apt to look spiritless and dull.

Much splendid work was produced in Italy at this period, but in such a wide field there are naturally some places that exhibit technique rather than art. The student must go into it with appreciative faculties alert lest mere splendor should sweep him off his feet.

The wares and the potters of Italy penetrated north into Europe, to France, the Holy Roman Empire and Britain, starting or stimulating what was to prove an overwhelming flood of production. In Europe in pre-Roman times, a coarse, unglazed, built-up ware was general, it being of simple, somewhat clumsy but vigorous form, low-fired and friable. It was used chiefly for cinerary purposes, the Germanic peoples having a decided preference for vessels of horn, wood, or metal.

The Romans introduced the wheel and produced a far higher class of ware. Their importation of the fine red Samian pottery resulted in the fabrication of the vigorous Gallo-Roman and Romano-British pottery. This was good in shape and paste and characteristically decorated with slip, bosses, dots, and indentations. The later Gaulish work shows applied figures and highly finished scroll work. After the decline of Rome, Saxon and Germanic work shows a distinctly retrograde tendency. It is often built up, strapped, banded, and bossed in imitation of the Romano-British. Though coarse and lacking in finish, it is full of freshness and character.

In Medieval England, when pottery making was at a low ebb, the monasteries and travelling guilds of potters produced splendid encaustic tiles. These were inlaid with simple yet striking geometric designs, or animal or bird forms, both heraldic and symbolic.

In Europe for many years the domestic pottery remained coarse and primitive, showing still the arresting hand of the barbarian conquerors of Rome. The first signs of the Italian Renaissance are to be found in the rare Henri Deux or Orion ware. Palissy's desperate and romantic search for enamels was the prelude to the development of Rouen, Nevers, Lille, Moustiers, Sèvres, Marseilles, and other less important potteries. In France also early experiments led eventually to the fabrication of porcelain much on the lines of English porcelain, a frit being used instead of kaolin.

In Germany, as early as the Fifteenth Century, they produced fine stoneware highly decorated with relief patterns and colors. After long research Boettiger, by a lucky accident, discovered kaolin. Porcelain was made at Dresden in 1709, and many of the Dresden figures show a remarkably sympathetic alliance of potting, modeling and painting.

The success of the German ceramists led to a wide patronage of potters by kings and princes which quickly spread the knowledge of porcelain throughout Europe.

Long before this in the early part of the Seventeenth Century, potteries were established at Delft in Holland. Here was made the well-known ware painted in blue camaien on a fine white ground. This was for a time produced in great quantities, and the process of painting directly on to an absorbent ground led to a surprisingly fresh and skillful style.

In the middle of the Seventeenth Century English wares commenced to rise from the stagnation in which they seemed sunk since Saxon times. Toft, with his tygs and platters, Dwight, and his bellarmines, and Elers, with turned shapes, started a movement which was eventually to send English wares into all parts of Europe, even into far Russia, to be known everywhere for its excellent workmanship. And in this flood of production in the Seventeenth and Eighteenth Centuries was much that was technically unrivalled despite the fact that the Art of the potter is sometimes far to seek. Dwight is said to have produced a fritted porcelain in 1671, before the discovery of kaolin. This is doubtful, but his persistent research eventually led up to the fine pastes of Chelsea and Bow and the unrivalled "fine earthenwares" of Staffordshire.

This European revival gained tremendous impetus from the importation by the Portuguese of the wares of China. The wide scope of its decoration, both painted and modeled, pointed the way to most potters of the West during the heyday of European pottery. The magnificent single-color pieces were not introduced until later when the break-up of the Empire rendered them accessible to Europeans. It is to them that the student must turn to see the summit of the potter's art, which, it is logically contended, commences on the wheel and ends at the glost oven with the potter, the only attendant from the pot's inception to its finish. Painting or modeling is not essential to its perfection and unless applied by a true disciple detracts rather than adds to the beauty of the piece.

In China, where tradition holds that earthenware was first made in 2698 B.C., the art of the potter, in body, shape, glaze, and color, through centuries reached perfection. Porcelain is said to have been first made about 200 B.C., but this date is conjectural. What we do know unmistakably, however, is that the best work of their best periods is unrivalled. Depending primarily on form and color, with here and there a subtle decoration in raised or incised line, in crackle or simple brushwork, it stands alone, and despite the omnipotent chemistry of today, defies imitation. Their forms are strong, bold, and dignified, yet subtle and delicate, too. Then, added to a wonderful range of colors, was a perfection of body that was for so long the despair of western imitators. It is here at the altar of perfection amidst the chaste richness of Tang and Sung and Ming that the true disciple must worship. And to those who must eat bread as well as make pots it is to be pointed out that these pieces at the time of their production fetched prices that compare favorably with the "fancy" prices given today.

To the Japanese also in great measure the same tribute is due. Although beginning later as disciples and scarcely getting so far as their masters, their more limited range of color and form is set off by their restrained and even more tasteful decoration. The unique collection in the Boston Museum is an amplification of this bald statement. They were often more concerned with the touch and texture of the pot than the more obvious appeal of decoration. Esoteric as it is to most occidentals it is rich in a pure æstheticism and a deep and beautiful symbolism that is slowly but surely having an influence on western art, just when it seems in some danger of dying out in Japan. The hermit kingdom of Korea, despite its midway position, produced pottery that is strangely beautiful and distinctive and worth much more than a passing notice.

In China the art decadence of the Eighteenth and Nineteenth Centuries, coupled with internal revolutions, has sadly dimmed her plots, dispersed her potters, and all but

George J. Cox

destroyed her priceless traditions.

For the further development of pottery in Europe and America and Asia the student has many excellent books to consult. From the Seventeenth Century the ramifications are rapid and all-embracing, giving, however, more joy to the collector than to the artist.

Modern work has made an enormous advance in the science of the craft. Since the "Eighties" it shows signs of a renaissance in æsthetics. Lusters of all shades, crystalline, star, and crackle glazes with safe methods of oxidizing and reducing in the fire, have been brought to perfection. Yet, with some few exceptions, commerce seems writ large upon them all and their very perfection of finish damns them in the eyes of an artist. Whichever way he looks, he must return again and again to refresh his eyes with the inspiring examples of the best that has survived from the near and far East.

Only an antiquarian humbug would wish to go back to ancient conditions even to produce old pots. But it is only by seeing in so far as we may in museums and books the works of these ancient yet ever modern potters; by tracing their development, appreciating their qualities and attempting to work as they worked, honestly and unaffectedly, that we shall begin to approach the excellence and originality of their art. This study should not of course obey the direction it all too frequently follows. The slavish measuring by module and fraction of classic styles, the stark geometric analysis of Moorish ornament or the laborious copying of Chinese pattern is at best only art in cold storage. It should be self-evident that where an alien style is consciously imitated the result is sterility for the imitator.

In others, it is apt to produce a powerful reaction that results in *Futurism* or some such self-conscious affectation. "The Greeks did not draw from casts nor did the Persians haunt museums," says the harried student. No. But better than that, they were surrounded, if not by beauty, at least by nature naked and unashamed. They lived not easily maybe, but surely more gracefully, untrammelled by fashion, cult, or craze.

"The earth his sober Inn
And quiet pilgrimage."

Their best work seems ever fresh, spontaneous, and untired. It must have been done with a spirit and real joy impossible to anyone but a true craftsman tremendously interested in his work, we might also add, his environment.

Naturally, present-day conditions must modify the struggle for existence. They may mar our best aim at times. Yet some few have worked wonders even in this age. To mention but two instances, W. De Morgan and the Martin brothers, is to tell of high endeavor and great achievement. But we must not expect to get rich that way.

Pottery is an exacting and difficult craft, abounding in as many trials and disappointments as excitements and rewards. Its true devotee must suffer. Yet the delightful tale of Palissy's heroic battle should hearten the more fortunate student of today. It is good to read of the spirit in which Wedgwood, scientist though he was, approached his work. In a trade catalogue he says, "A Competition for Cheapness, and not for Excellence of Workmanship, is the most frequent cause of rapid Decay and entire Destruction of Art and of Manufacture." "Beautiful Forms are not to be made by Chance and they never were made nor can be made in any kind at small expense." Such sentiments rarely emanate from the modern commercial pottery.

Tradition, except the traditions of flawless glazes, certain soulless results, and commercial cheese paring; seems dead perhaps, but it will surely come to life again. To see the potter "thumping his wet clay," and seated at the wheel of ancient lineage, conjuring forth a wealth of gracious shapes, is to renew one's faith in the ultimate survival of simple honest handicraft even in this machine-ridden age. Masterpieces were never conceived in factories, and when we make pots primarily for love of them, not to sell them, we shall begin to beat back the manufacturer of debauched "Art" pots into that domestic and hygienic realm wherein his efforts are particularly admirable and effective. A craft that teems with such an endless variety of beautiful objects for such countless uses can never remain for all time the handmaiden of commerce.

Basics of ... Pottery

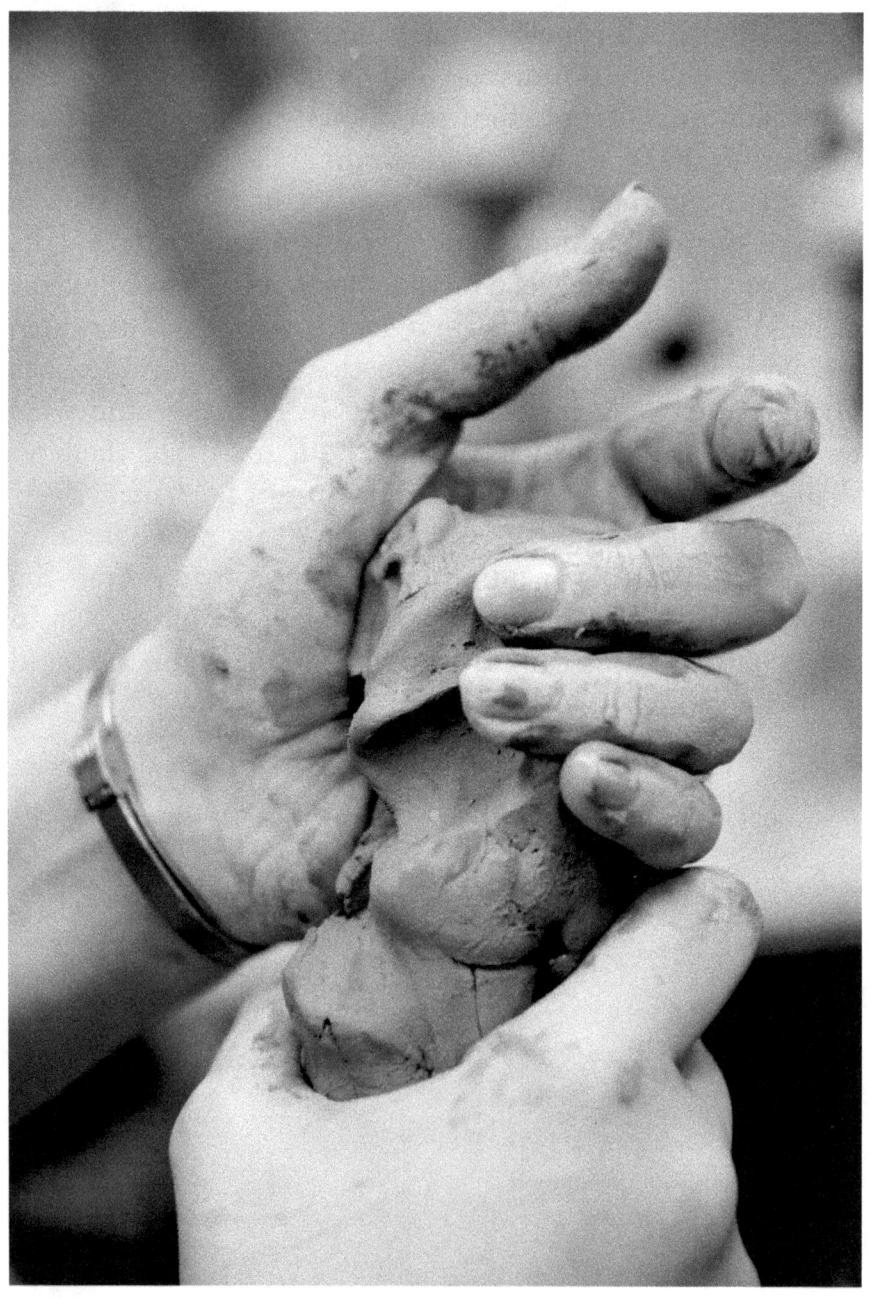

CHAPTER II
Clays and Pastes

"It is the Art which gives the value, and not the material."
—Dresser.

Clay being the chief material used by the potter, it demands a description which, without being too technical, will give from the start a clear idea of the nature of clays or pastes in general use.

It would be a needless complication to enter here into a discussion of the chemical analysis of bodies and materials. Whilst the chemist can and does determine with exactitude the relative quantities of each component, he cannot yet, let us perhaps be thankful, lay down with the same certainty the structural and molecular changes all these compounds will undergo in the fire. The old potters' rule "of thumb" or, rather, common sense and experience, still count for something.

Clay is the word generally applied to the natural article when used without preparation, or after picking and washing. Paste is the term used for all composite bodies that have been through a complicated process of washing, grinding, mixing, and sieving, or even fritting, according to the desired quality of the ware for which it is required. Natural clays range from the pure white and very infusible kaolin, containing only alumina and silica with a very small percentage of alkalis, to the impure grey, red, or brown clays, containing, along with alumina and silica, magnesia, potash, soda, iron, lime, and carbon. Kaolin is used with China stone (a combination of feldspar and quartz) to make porcelain, the finest and hardest paste known to potters. It has a very hard white translucent body, only slightly vitreous at the highest fire (around 1700° Centigrade).

From this, the highest grade, we have almost insensible gradations to common earthenware. Old English and French porcelain were compounded of clay, sand, and alkalis ground together to make a frit, re-ground and mixed with a stiffening material (in English porcelain, bone-ash), to support the vitreous matter in the intense heat. The finest earthenware does not differ greatly in its formula from soft porcelain, but it is not so hard or transparent. From this the scale descends to where the presence of lime or iron in the body color it and render it easily fusible, so that at any great heat it turns black and collapses to a slag.

Clay on being dug up is usually weathered in the open, and dried and broken up and the greater impurities picked out. It is then thoroughly mixed with water in a blunger and passed through a succession of sieves until all foreign matter and impurities are left behind and it is the consistency of cream. This was formerly done by hand, the clay being raked into a thick "slub" and washed through a series of tanks until all impurities had settled, leaving only the fine clay in suspension. It is at this stage that any additions are made to form a paste. The modifying ingredients, ground and sieved to the requisite degree, are thoroughly incorporated with the slip, which is allowed to settle. The clear water on top is siphoned off and the paste dried sufficiently to handle. The modern method of preparation is to force the slip through a series of straining bags which remove most of the water and leave it stiff enough to work. Some of the hard pastes are so stiff or short that they require soap water to give plasticity, but usually after a thorough wedging it is now ready for the thrower.

Generally speaking, kaolin, China clay, ball clay, pipe clay, China stone, feldspar, flint, quartz, sand, lime, chalk, and calcined bone are the ingredients of most modern pastes. These supply the alumina, silica, lime, potash, and soda, with traces of iron and magnesia, that are found in all clays when analyzed. Carbon is only present in impure bodies fired at a low heat.

Of these materials the clays rich in alumina and silica, such as kaolin or China clay, form the body-giving substance. The feldspar or China stone furnish the fluxing ingredients for fusing and binding. The flint or bone supplies the stiffening matter for supporting and retaining the shape of the object in the fire.

Porcelain, though differing so widely in appearance and texture from the coarse medieval earthenware or the pottery of the ancients, is found to have a distinct relationship when all these bodies are submitted to analysis. Much of the difference in bodies, apart from the impurities, lies in the temperature of the fire to which it has been submitted. At a low temperature such constituents as lime and iron are not much affected, but at a greater heat they act as fluxing agents.

To generalize upon a complex and difficult subject one might say that porcelain, both hard and soft (pâte dure and pâte tendre), is characterized by its pure white color and by extreme hardness of body and glaze with transparency; fine stoneware by a very hard, opaque, and heavy body which may be white, buff, or grey, and salt-glazed or with a fine hard transparent glaze. Earthenware is softer and mostly opaque. It may range from something a little softer than soft porcelain to the coarse "Majolica" with a tin glaze, differing widely in color of body and hardness of glaze.

With porcelain and the finest high-fired wares a purity of materials and uniformity of mass is absolutely necessary. It is here that one may well call in the aid of the chemist and manufacturer. In any case it is advisable to call in the chemist and the manufacturer when working on a large scale. With a small output, as with all good craftsmen, the fabrication of a good, reliable stoneware or earthenware paste is only a matter of patience and hard work. Before commencing to produce finished work on any scale, repeated experiments with different clays should be carried out. Notes of all trials, with and without glaze, are invaluable to the potter.

Rich clays can be stiffened, short clays enriched, and color modified without a mass of expensive machinery. Rich, easily fusible clays tend to *stunt* or buckle at a high fire. Hard refractory clays often remain porous and are a fruitful source of crazing and breaking. The addition of flint or fine washed sand, finely powdered *grog*, or *pitchers*, or even refractory China clays, in quantities varying from about 5 per cent to 20 per cent, but settled only by repeated trials, will stiffen up or open out rich clays inclined to warp or burst. Rich fusible clays added to hard clays may stop the crazing, or the fusing point may be lowered by the addition of spar. Stiff gravelly clay will require finer sieving or repeated washing to rid it of some of the grit or sand. Rich greasy clays are better when not too finely sieved, but this point is of course dependent on the class of work to be undertaken. Slip can be settled in tubs, the water siphoned off, and then put to dry on plaster bats, or dry clay, powdered and sieved, may be stirred in until the mass is stiff enough to wedge thoroughly by hand.

In mixing or modifying without machinery it is sometimes advisable to do it in the dry state, otherwise some of the heavier materials are likely to sink and are thus not thoroughly incorporated with the body. The dry mass when well mixed is wetted enough to be wedged. When the body is colored and a white ground is indispensable, an "engobe," or dip, of white clay slip must be resorted to.

These processes are certainly tedious, but that will not deter a craftsman searching for the right clay in which best to shape his ideas. To the craftsman working alone it is the only way by which he can accommodate his clays to the various necessities of throwing, casting, or modeling. Each process will require a slightly different nature in the clay if the finest results are to be obtained.

Although in this craft book we shall not approach porcelain, a good, hard, true-ringing body with a tough well-fitting glaze should be a *sine qua non* with all craftsmen; and it is only in the fire that any true idea can be gained of the important influences clays and pastes have on the finished work. Here we have tried to indicate the chief characteristics of clays and to make clear the inevitable tendency of all potters who seek an imperishable medium for their craft towards a purer body and a higher fire.

Basics of ... Pottery

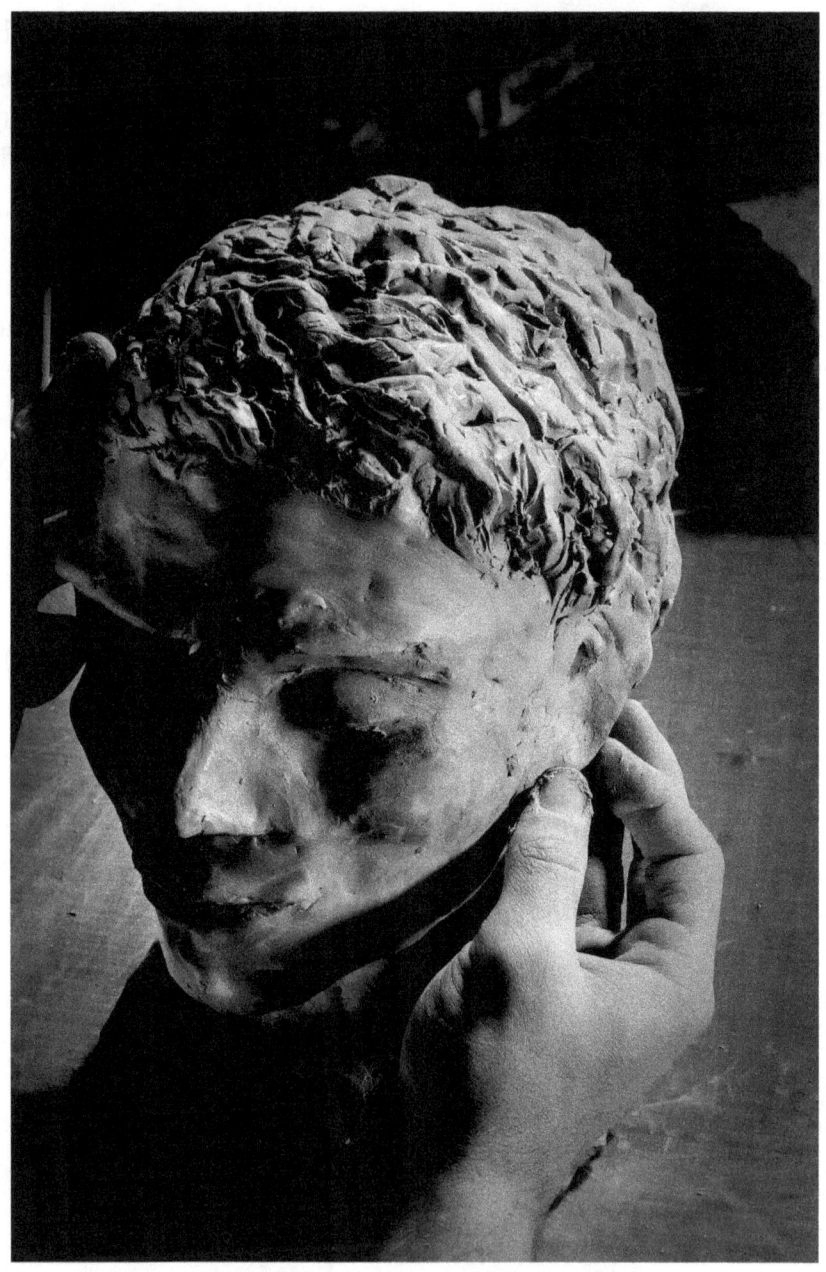

CHAPTER III
Built Shapes

"Every moment think steadily: to do what thou hast in hand with perfect and simple dignity."
—M. Antoninus

With good plastic clay and with the aid of a few simple tools, the fingers can fashion shapes of considerable diversity and some refinement. In elementary schools this is by far the best method of teaching the beginner. In any case the student who has no knowledge of clay work would do well to start by building a few shapes in the manner still used by primitive peoples.

The clay, which must be in good condition and not *short*, is rolled out on a wet plaster slab or some non-sticky surface, into ropes of something less than half an inch in diameter for small shapes. The best way to commence is to knead up a double handful of soft clay until thoroughly mixed, ball it, and then form a stumpy cylinder, gradually elongating by rolling out on the bat. Too much pressure will flatten the rope and there should be a distinct pull or stretch on it in addition to the downward pressure, varying as necessary to insure even thickness. As the rope becomes thinner the fingers should be held diagonally to avoid ridges. This rope should be fairly firm and yet bend easily without cracking. With a little practice, long pliable rolls can be easily and rapidly produced and then a start is made with the base.

This is coiled, pressed flat, and welded together. It is finished both sides before commencing the walls of the shape. These are coiled round and up, each ring being pressed firmly on the one below, care being taken to avoid air cavities which may blow out on firing. The top is leveled off and the sides welded together and smoothed with the fingers.

At first, simple and almost straight-sided shapes should be attempted; each ring may be added separately, while the finishing should not be unduly prolonged. As the technique improves, curves with slight returns may be attained. Where the size is so great as to prevent finishing at one sitting, it can be very carefully reversed; this will allow the base to harden and still keep the top moist for further coiling. With big pieces much attention must be paid to the correct shaping when coiling, otherwise the finishing will be laborious and quite possibly useless. Large shapes with difficult curves are best built in two sections or parts and then carefully welded together. To keep the parts damp during prolonged operations, use water blown from a spray diffuser.

Ash trays, bulb bowls, flower pots, salt cellars, and ink wells are a few of the things that are suitable to be made by this method. They may be decorated with incised lines, raised-ornament handles, and feet. Additional interest is obtained by slight banding, or the incised lines filled in with a colored clay pressed firmly in when the shape is tough. Although built forms may be quite highly finished, it is obvious that any elaborate decoration is out of place on shapes that by their origin must be simple and somewhat heavy. Enough has been said to indicate the process. For its logical development and suitable enrichment we must study the work of primitive peoples. For its possibilities we must turn to the vast jars made even to this day in Spain.

With great care and much taste pieces can be pinched and welded together into delightful forms, best shown in the refinements of the Cha Noya pottery of Japan. This pinching must be done carefully and above all sympathetically. To those that know or feel the possibilities of the clay it will respond readily. Much more taste and judgment is required in the making of a really satisfactory pinched shape, than is needed in forming one with coils. Square, polyhedral, or irregular shapes other than circular may be *stuck up* or pieced together in the following manner: Upon a table nail two strips of wood one quarter of an inch thick, ten or twelve inches apart. Sprinkle between the strips with flint or fine sand and batter out some soft clay thereon. Scrape the surplus clay off with a straight-edge and then roll the clay between the strips flat with a rolling pin. Upon this thin slab mark out the sides, base, top, etc., of the shape to be built. Run a thin knife round each shape, but do not cut quite down to the table. Cut along the inside edge of each strip to allow the whole slab to contract evenly and allow it to toughen slightly. Carefully remove and reverse the slab and separate the pieces, being careful not to distort the shapes in the process.

The shape must be stuck up before the pieces become brittle or too stiff to bend. Roughen each opposing edge and moisten with slip, that is, clay mixed with water to the consistency of thick cream.

Press the edges firmly together and weld well each joint with soft clay. This operation should be most thorough, as any weak joint will inevitably open when fired. Lids should be cut slightly larger than the shapes they have to fit and sandpapered true when dry. Sharp edges and angles should be smoothed with the fingers before the shape gets hard.

The chief pitfall to avoid in this process is a hard wooden look. The ductile plastic qualities of the clay should be remembered and such additions as feet or handles should emphasize this important point.

Finally, the careful sympathetic craftsman, with infinite patience, by utilizing all three methods, can build vessels of almost any shape,—square, round, elliptical, banded, strapped, bossed, fluted, and embellished with handles, spouts, and feet. Ancient and medieval pottery is rich in such forms.

Basics of ... Pottery

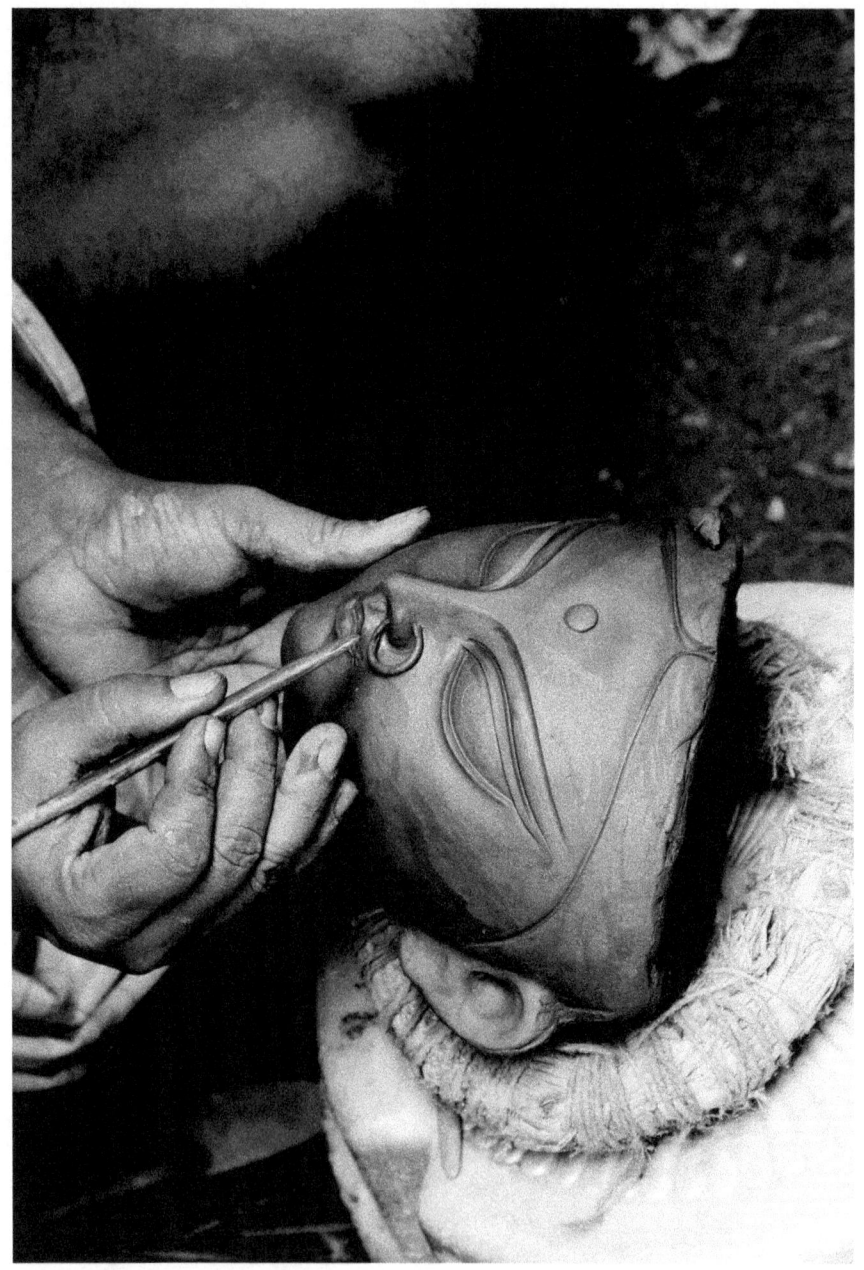

CHAPTER IV
Molding, Casting, and Pressing

*"Our soundes is good, Our shapes is neat,
Its Davis cast us so compleat."*
—From an old bell at Stoke Rivers

The casting process, employed so extensively in commercial work, is in its essence mechanical and therefore can never have the spontaneity or character of thrown work. Today when the thrower and turner with hand and eye trained for good shapes is rare indeed, it is often the only method by which the student can obtain large shapes of high finish for painting or glazing in transparent colors.

In the process the shape is first designed and carefully drawn on paper, allowance being made for the shrinkage of the finished pot which may be as much as 1 in 6 with some kinds of slip. It should be refined in profile with no returns that may bind or hold in the mold when drying, yet it is obvious that simple shapes that can be built or thrown by the beginner are not suitable for casting.

The shape correctly drawn, a mandrel, a steel tapering to a point, the butt wormed to screw on a lathe, and long enough to give some play at either end, is rolled in stout paper, gummed at the edges. This is removed and allowed to set, thus giving a paper shell just fitting the mandrel. Trim this square at the base and stick it upright by means of a piece of clay on a well-oiled portion of a table. Around this as a center is fitted a roll of linoleum, oiled inside and secured with string, with all its joints caulked with clay. The inside diameter of this cylinder should be about ½" larger than the greatest diameter of the drawn shape. Enough superfine plaster to fill this is now mixed. To do this shake plaster by handfuls into a bowl of water until it appears to refuse more, pour off any surplus water, and stir with a wooden ladle or the hand, avoiding air bubbles.

A little practice in casting plaster bats will give the experience necessary for mixing plaster. When well mixed and a slight thickening is perceptible, it is poured very carefully into the cylinder, the paper shell being kept upright in the center. In about 20 minutes the surface of the plaster will feel warm. It is now set and the linoleum is removed. The plaster cylinder, when dry, is fitted on the mandrel, and this screwed to the lathe head. Two or three chisels are now required. The rest on the lathe is clamped in a convenient position and a cutting chisel held as shown, cutting edge up. The cylinder is revolved briskly as indicated by arrow, and the shape is roughly hollowed out. Proceed gradually until the shape begins to emerge, taking care not to cut too deeply. Towards the finish use the calipers frequently to check the measurements.

At top and bottom about ½" waste is left, turned straight, the actual line of top and base being slightly grooved in the plaster. The form may be pretty accurately finished with the chisels and then nicely smoothed with sandpaper. For this process the rotary movement is reversed.

The shape is now removed from the lathe and is ready for molding.

With a kick wheel having a removable head the mandrel

can be screwed on and the block turned down in an upright position. The difficulty of steadying the tool renders this method somewhat unsuitable for this process, where perfect symmetry and a high finish are required. The plaster should not be so dense for turning on the wheel or the kicking is apt to become very arduous and this tends to dislocate the set of the spindle. One of the best of ways is to draw a quantity of shapes, cast their blocks, and turn them on a hired lathe, preferably run by power.

The finished shape is now well lathered with parting or stopping. This is made by boiling 1 lb. soft soap, 1/4 lb. Russian tallow, and a small piece of soda. Another stopping is made by dissolving 1 lb. soft soap in 1 qt. water and stirring in 1/4 pt. paraffin oil. Several coatings may be necessary to impart a waxy surface. When no longer absorbent, it is dried and slightly polished with a bit of cotton waste. At the finish the form should be clean, smooth, glossy, and non-absorbent.

With simple shapes, a one-piece or a two-piece mold can be made, and here the bottom waste is not necessary, but with any return or foot a three-piece mold will be required. The waxed shape is now divided perpendicularly exactly in half, by a pencil line. It is then laid on its side and bedded in clay up to the pencil lines, the clay being sloped slightly down from the marks. Box in now with well-soaped boards tight against top and bottom but allowing about 1 1/2" at sides. Wipe the shape over with waste dipped in olive oil but leave no surplus oil on the surface. Plaster well mixed as before is poured in until about 1 1/2" to 2" above the greatest projection of the shape, great care being taken to avoid or dislodge air bubbles.

When the plaster is set but still warm, the shape is removed and the side of the plaster that rested on the clay trimmed flat and several joggles or natches are made. The shape is now replaced exactly as cast and the new surfaces treated with parting and the whole slightly filmed with oil as before. Great care must be used, for any oil on the actual surface of the mold spoils the suction of the plaster at that spot. Box in and then cast just as before. This gives two halves with waste top and bottom.

The shape is now placed on the lathe and the bottom waste turned off, the base of the shape being slightly hollowed. The creator having arrived so far successfully may now unbend and scratch his mark on this new surface before well waxing it.

Dowels are cut in the waste of the two halves as shown, the fresh parts soaped, all fitted together and slightly oiled, then boxed in. Plaster about 2" thick at the thinnest part is poured on and the mold is complete. When set, the shape is removed and the three parts trimmed on all the outside edges. The three pieces are assembled, firmly tied up to prevent warping, and thoroughly dried.

If preferred, the mold can be made cylindrical instead of square. This will give a more even suction to the slip and may be worth the extra trouble. For casting purposes a refractory clay containing a good percentage of China clay, maturing at about 03-01 but remaining perfectly white and porous, will be required.

Slip for casting is made thus: Clay, picked or broken into small pieces, is thrown into a bucket of warm water well slubbed up by hand and passed through a fine sieve (No. 80) with the aid of a stout brush and thinned to the consistency of thick cream. This should be matured for some days, frequently stirred, and again sieved before using. For very small or fragile shapes, a finer sieve (120) is advisable. The mold, quite dry and clean, is now slightly moistened with a scrupulously clean sponge and water, the parts assembled, corded, and firmly wedged, leaving the top free. The slip, thoroughly stirred, is poured in very gently to avoid bubbles. With awkward molds, a tube or funnel should be used to prevent splashing. If the mold be placed on a whirler and turned to and fro, it will prevent the heavier matter in the slip settling too quickly.

As the slip sinks in the mold, the subsidence being due to the absorption of the water by the plaster, the mold should be continually filled up. After a few minutes the mouth is scraped free to test the deposit. When this is thick enough, varying, of course, with the size of the shape, the slip is poured out into another bucket. An unorthodox but often useful trick for strengthening long necks is to slide a piece of glass over the mouth and reverse the mold for a minute or so. The neck full of slip thus allows a slight extra deposit on the part that most needs it when we come to finishing off the lip.

Let the mold drain a little over the slip bucket and then reverse to dry slowly. When the wet look has disappeared from the surface of the slip, scrape the top free and run a knife around to prevent sticking as the shape contracts. In a few hours it will be dry enough to permit of the sides being eased off and the shape left to dry on the base. When tough enough to handle with safety, the waste and cast lines are trimmed and finished off, any air bubbles or holes broken down and filled with clay scraped from the waste or base. If this finishing is left until the shape be dry, it is impossible to hide such defects. The greatest care must be exercised in handling cast shapes, as they are exceptionally fragile.

When quite dry, the whole form should be carefully gone over with a very fine sandpaper. A superfine surface should be imparted by rubbing with the hands. When using transparent glazes, as with under-glaze painting, it is essential that all scratches be removed, and especially must all sharp edges be eliminated on neck or shoulder, for the glaze running away from these places imparts a hideously cheap look to what otherwise may be a fine shape. All these points having received attention, the date is scratched on the bottom of the shape and it is now ready to biscuit.

Generally speaking, it will be found that slip the consistency of cream is right for casting, possibly thicker for big open shapes, and after the right proportion is settled it is as well to test what it weighs to the pint.

As will be readily seen, this process, whilst open to many objections, lends itself to shapes that are refined and delicate and to those that have flutings or raised ornament. Such decorations, or the spouts of jugs, may be modeled in wax on the plaster shape before casting and appear in reverse on the mold. Designs may be scratched on the mold or shape and show as a delicate tracery beneath the glaze. All these things, however, add to the difficulty of casting and should be approached by degrees and with restraint. For in unskilled hands the process lends itself to soulless and mechanical repetition.

Pressing

Molds having moderately wide mouths enable the potter

to press his shapes instead of cast them.

This method in expert hands is even quicker than casting and has the advantage of imparting a sturdier look to large shapes. Pressing is also resorted to for those shapes to which it would be difficult for the slip to obtain free access.

For the ordinary three-piece mold the procedure would be thus: The clay, well wedged and quite plastic, is rolled out as described in Jigger and Jolley work, to a suitable thickness. Butter cloth or fine linen will do instead of leather to roll the clay on. The insides of the three parts of the mold are sponged and pieces of the thin rolled clay roughly cut to fit them.

These pieces are now fitted and well applied to the three parts by dabbing with the damp sponge. A soft close-textured sponge, or a soft felt dabber, is best for this operation. When closely setting, the edges are trimmed and given a slight bevel. The top is cut straight. Then the mold is assembled and firmly tied. Some of the waste clay is rolled into thin *ropes*. With the beveled edges slightly moistened, these ropes are firmly wedged into the two side junctions and round the base. Where the mouth is large enough for the insertion of the hand this is not a difficult operation. If it be narrow, the two halves of the mold may be tied up and the joints welded together before they are assembled on the base. A coil of clay can then be placed on the edge of the base just clear of the two sides which are now fitted over and tied up. Then a stick sponge is used to join up the base to the sides. After a little while the shape is fit to be removed and is finished in the usual way.

Nothing can rival large thrown shapes for vigor or variety, but unfortunately they are not always within reach of even the good craftsman. Then this method offers the least objectionable substitute for them and in clever hands is capable of many fine results.

The following method is used to mold handles or simple applied ornament. Handles, feet, masks, etc., are usually pressed and stuck on the dry shape with slip. To mold them some skill is necessary if the press is to be quite accurate and free from twist or ugly seams.

One way, when the handle or foot is symmetrical, is to cut the model exactly in half. This must be done when the model is tough enough to handle without bending or distorting it. One half is laid cut side down upon a sheet of glass, and surrounded at a convenient distance with clay walls. Plaster is now poured on to form one half of the mold, and allowed to set. It is then removed and the smooth surface joggled and claywashed (brushed over with claywater). The other half is then very carefully applied to the half still embedded in the mold, the walls built round and the other part of the mold cast. Then all is trimmed up and a groove run round the form as shown. For pressing, the form is well filled with clay and the two halves of the mold strongly pressed together. Any surplus clay will squeeze into the groove and when tough enough to remove the whole is "fettled" and finished before drying and sticking up.

With care and practice this method is possible: Build walls and pour in enough plaster to form one half of the mold. Before it stiffens, very carefully press in the handle or ornament just up to the halfway line and allow to set. Joggle, claywash, and cast the second half. Finally, when the object is of any size, clay walls may be used as described in the chapter on Figurines.

Basics of ... Pottery

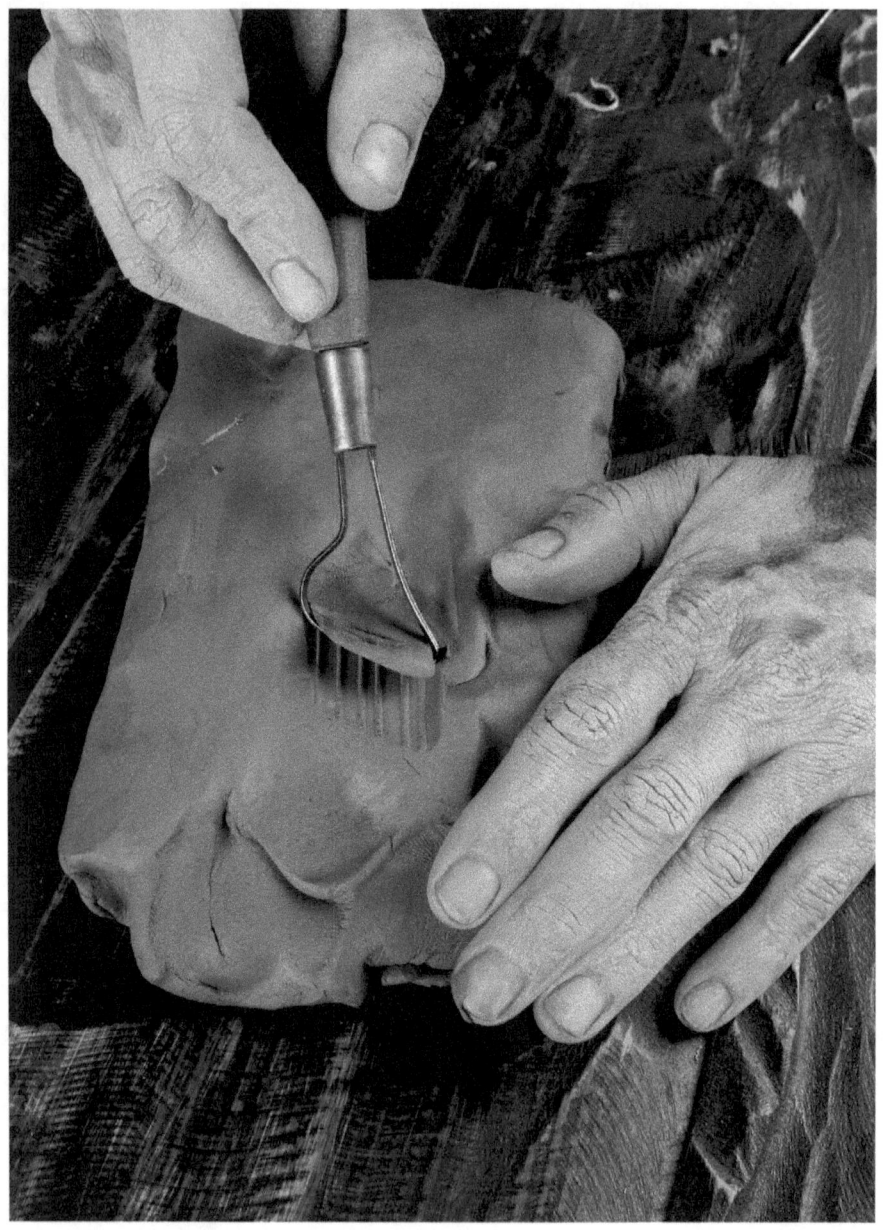

CHAPTER V
Jigger and Jolley Work

"Earth I am, et is most trwe, desdan me not, for so ar you."
—From an old platter

Dishes, platters, and to some extent bowls, are usually made on a *Jigger and Jolley*. The jigger has a revolving head, fitted to receive molds. The jolley has a pivoted arm to which different profiles may be clamped. In factories these things are complicated and go by power, but in a studio where the output of platters and dishes is likely to be limited something simple will do. Where the wheel is strong, well-hung, and fitted with a removable head, a contrivance as shown at Fig. 21 can be fitted by any carpenter, that should serve all purposes.

The vertical supports of the jolley arm should be quite rigid. The arm itself must so pivot that the face of any profile screwed onto it will cross the head of the jigger, or wheel if one be used, through the center. In other words, the cutting profile must form a diagonal of the circular head. Then, too, it must be hung at a height sufficient to allow a fairly thick block of plaster being used for a mold.

head or the jigger head is removed and soaped or oiled. Then a circular block of plaster is cast to fit. This may be done with the aid of a roll of linoleum, much in the way described in casting. The paper cone will, of course, be replaced by the wheel head, bedded face up in clay. This

Basics of ... Pottery

plaster block has to be molded to the exact size of the dish or plaque required. To do this a profile of zinc is necessary. The true section of the dish is drawn full size, and profiles giving one half of the back and front are traced on a stout sheet of zinc. The zinc is roughly cut to shape with shears and then finished with a file to a chisel edge (see cut). The two profiles are then firmly backed with shaped wooden forms, slotted to screw onto the arm of the jolley. The profile giving the *face* of the plaque is securely adjusted in a horizontal position, the inner point, giving the center of the platter, being exactly over the center of the jigger head. The plaster block, which should be turned down before it sets hard, is shipped back into position, the jigger revolved and the profile gradually pressed down until the true section is obtained, *i.e.* when the profile is exactly horizontal again. The mold is now removed, trimmed at the sides if necessary, and set apart to dry. It is then ready to use.

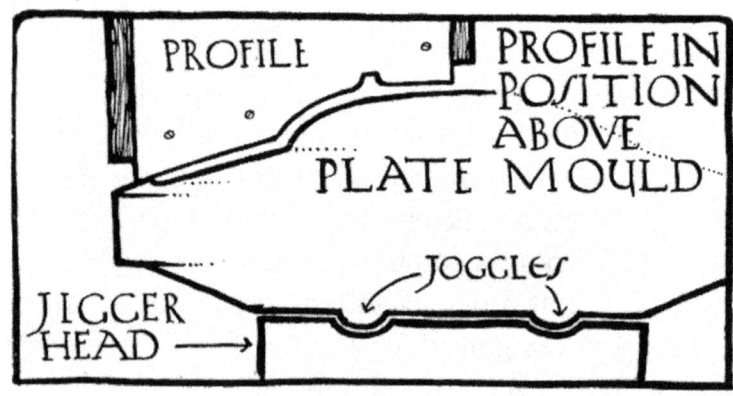

Fig. 22

The mold is slipped into position and revolved to insure even rotation. Then the profile giving the back of the platter screwed onto the arm and both adjusted until the stop allows the profile to rest at just that distance from the mold required by the thickness of the platter. (Fig. 22.)

The arm is then swung clear of the mold, which is well sponged with water to receive the clay. This is carefully wedged and then rolled out or batted flat on a piece of leather until it is a little thicker than the thickest part of the platter (see Fig. 23). The slab so made is smoothed with a palette knife, taken up, leather and all, slapped onto the mold, clay side down, and the leather removed. The clay is now well dabbed down with a wet sponge or dabber, to take out all wrinkles, pressed firmly onto the mold and the waste cut off.

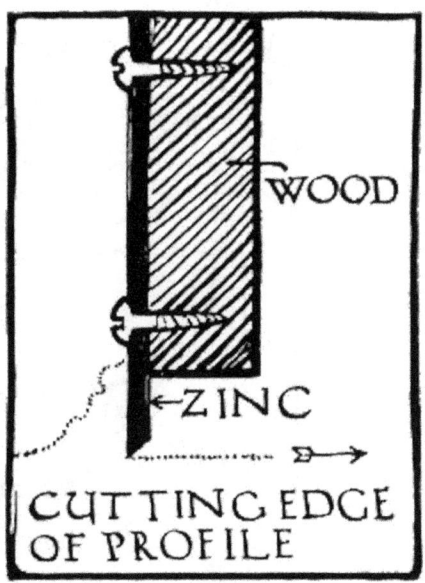

Fig. 23

Now the jigger or head is set spinning, the jolley pulled over it, and the profile gently pressed into the clay. Water is used freely to prevent the profile sticking, and as it becomes clogged the clay is removed. The turning is continued until the profile comes to a stop on the rest. Holes that may appear should be filled up before the finish, at which time the surface should present a smooth unscratched appearance. The shape is allowed to dry on the mold until tough enough to be slipped face down onto a perfectly flat slab dusted with fine sand or flint to prevent sticking. In this position it is left to dry, when the edges are nicely trimmed with fine sandpaper.

Fig. 24

For bowls the process is similar, but the mold here gives the outside and the profile the inside as in cut. (Fig. 24.) If made on the outside, they split before they can be removed. With small bowls the clay is wedged and a lump pressed into the mold by hand. With large bowls requiring a deep foot this must be turned separately and stuck on after the bowl is removed from the mold.

Where a jigger and jolley is not available, plates and bowls may be duplicated as follows: Place the plate bottom up on a well-soaped surface or a piece of glass. Should the plate not lie quite flat, caulk the apertures with clay, then all round and distant one and one half inches from the rim, build clay walls, or fix a containing band of linoleum, of sufficient height to allow plaster being poured in an inch and a half above the base or foot of the model. Mix fairly stiff plaster and pour in. Let it set, and then remove walls and the model. This gives a mold of the reverse of the plate or bowl.

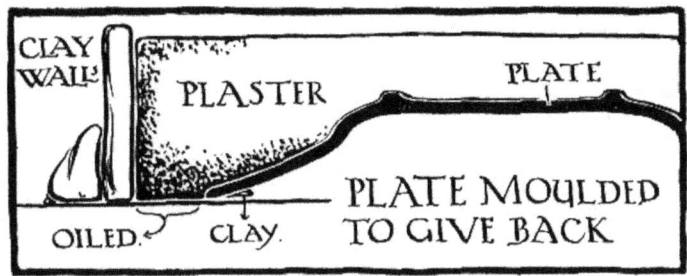

Fig. 25

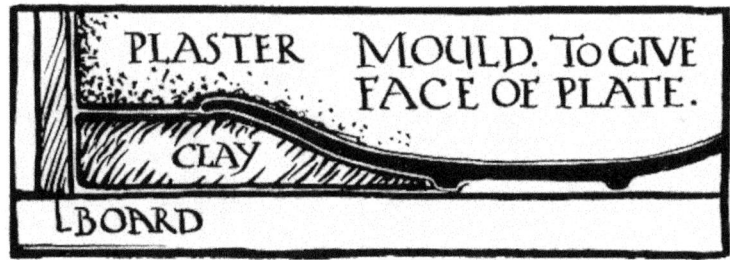

Fig. 26

Basics of ... Pottery

The mold is thoroughly dried before using and then sponged with clean water. Clay of the desired thickness is then rolled out as described and applied to the mold and dabbed flat with a sponge or dabber. The finish is imparted with the fingers and the surplus at edges trimmed with a knife. When tough, the press is slipped out and reversed to dry on a piece of sanded glass. Where there is a rim to the plate or bowl, this should be filled in cleanly with clay before the whole is pressed. It is of course impossible to mold thus bowls that possess a deep or under-cut foot.

George J. Cox

Basics of ... Pottery

Egypt. B.C. 2000

Basics of ... Pottery

CHAPTER VI
Thrown Shapes

"The lyf so short, the craft so longe to learne."
—Chaucer

The wheel is the true fountain head of all beautiful shapes, and the student who would become a potter cannot get "on the wheel" too soon. Throwing, sometimes *spinning*, is the term applied to the making of shapes on the wheel. Interesting and really fine pots may be built or cast, but the ultimate appeal rests with the thrown shape.

Unfortunately, a complete mastery of throwing is not to be gained by a few spasmodic wrestles with the wheel. It comes only with long hours of concentrated effort. Having watched an accomplished thrower and seen the full round shapes rise so easily between his dexterous fingers, it is with a severe shock that one realizes at the first attempt the skill and practice that will be required before such a desirable proficiency is attained.

The best kind of wheel is the kick wheel shown in the illustration. With this the feet, hands, and head work in harmony, accelerating or retarding the motions as required. It is a not distant relation of the earliest wheel, which was a heavy head on a short shaft, pivoted in a stone socket. Set spinning by hand, it was kept revolving some time by its own momentum. This form of wheel is used even to this day in the near and far East.

Basics of ... Pottery

Its first development was a secondary wheel and driving band turned by hand. This led to the wheel shown in the frontispiece and to the kick wheel and again on to the factory wheel. This in its turn is being superseded by the steam wheel, which gears onto a running band, the foot being used to start, stop, and regulate the speed. The two last named were introduced with the idea of accelerating the production rather than the improvement of the shapes. No doubt the now primitive kick wheel, much as used by the potters of the Renaissance, will be found good enough for us.

The tools required for throwing, after the wheel itself is secured, are as follows: a thin copper wire twisted between two bits of wood, a pricker, a fine soft sponge, another bit of sponge tied to a stick, one or two modeling tools and a rib (see Fig. 27).

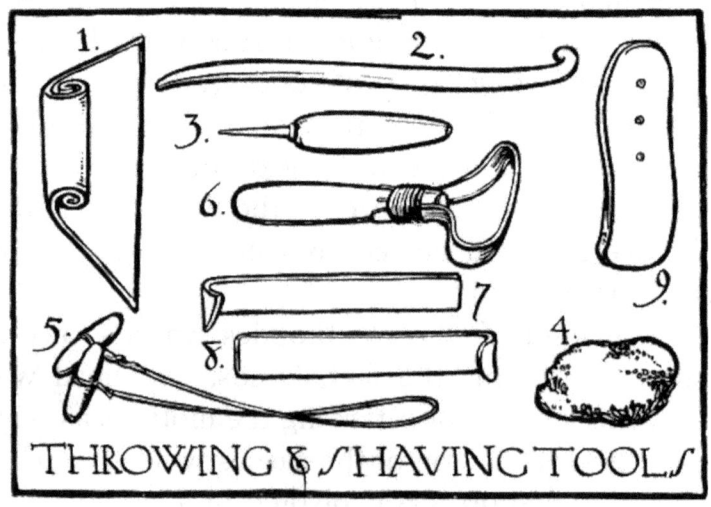

Fig. 27—1 "Rib"; 2, Modeling Tools; 3, Pricker; 4, Sponge; 5, Wire; 6, 7, and 8, Shaving Tools; 9, Leather.

George J. Cox

The clay is first knocked up into shape ready for the throwing. To do this it is *wedged*, a fair-sized piece being taken in both hands and thrown violently down on the bench, cut across, and smashed together again. This process is repeated until all air bubbles are expelled. This is ascertained by cutting with a wire. The finger is then passed across the surface to tell if it is well together, and not hard and soft in streaks. If, as must happen in a small pottery, the clay is out of condition, it is best remedied by cutting it with the wire into thin slabs, piling them crisscross and then wedging the mass. If still streaky, it can be quickly tempered, piece by piece. A double handful is torn across, wedged together at a different angle between the hands, re-torn, and re-wedged, until hard and soft are welded indistinguishably together.

This thorough wedging is essential, as with beginners a small lump or bubble will usually be sufficient to bring about the collapse of the shape.

The clay being thoroughly wedged is rolled into balls of a convenient size. For first practice they should be on the small side and moderately tough, as this allows a little more play before the ball becomes too soft. The wheel is now started revolving from right to left (see cut). The head being clean, the ball is thrown smartly onto its center. The hands are now wetted in a bowl of water, which is put, together with the tools, on the shelf to the right. Then gently but firmly, with hands placed as shown in Fig. 28, the ball is centered. At this stage, perhaps the most critical of all, the wheel should revolve quite briskly. The hands should be moistened if inclined to stick and the left hand held steady, the elbow pressed into the side, the forearm hard on the rest.

Basics of ... Pottery

The right hand has more freedom and coaxes the ball into a half sphere. This when dead centered is elongated, pressed down again, and re-formed into a truncated cone. The left hand still steadying, the thumb of the right is pressed firmly into the center of the top, down and out, to hollow the ball (see page 18), but stopping short of the lathe head. At this stage the most convenient shape to form is a cylinder, its walls gradually diminishing upwards with a little fatness at the rim. To do this the wheel is slowed down a little and the fingers of the left hand inserted. The sides are felt and gently pulled up, between the left index finger and the two first fingers of the right hand, gradually higher and thinner, always endeavoring to keep the walls at an even but slightly tapering thickness. (Fig. 29.)

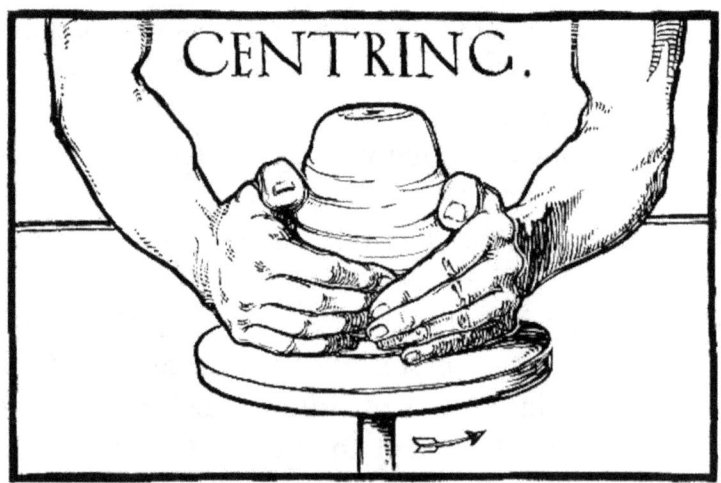

Fig. 28

Fig. 29

At first two fingers only will be inserted, but as the shapes grow in size the whole of the left hand will gain admittance. Then the perfect cylinder may be modified to almost any required form. With narrow-mouthed shapes the opening must be kept as small as possible, for the clay once pulled out it is difficult if not impossible to compress it again. The centering and hollowing once mastered, the chief difficulties to avoid are getting the bottom of the walls too thin before the top is pulled up, and making the top wavy and irregular. If the latter happens, it should be at once cut back with the pricker, which is also used to test the thickness of the sides and base.

When the shape has been pulled up to the required form and is sufficiently thin, the top is smoothed and fattened between the fingers. This not only imparts a look of substance to the vase and takes away any *cast* look, but gives strength where it is most needed. The inside, if wet, can be cleaned out with the stick sponge and the outside lightly smoothed with the other sponge. For the insides of bowls or wide-mouthed shapes, a rib of slate or zinc (see Fig. 30) will be useful for obliterating ridges. The last operation is to pass the wire, held firmly to the wheel head, beneath the pot and lift it off and place it on one of the pot boards or plaster discs. (Fig. 32.)

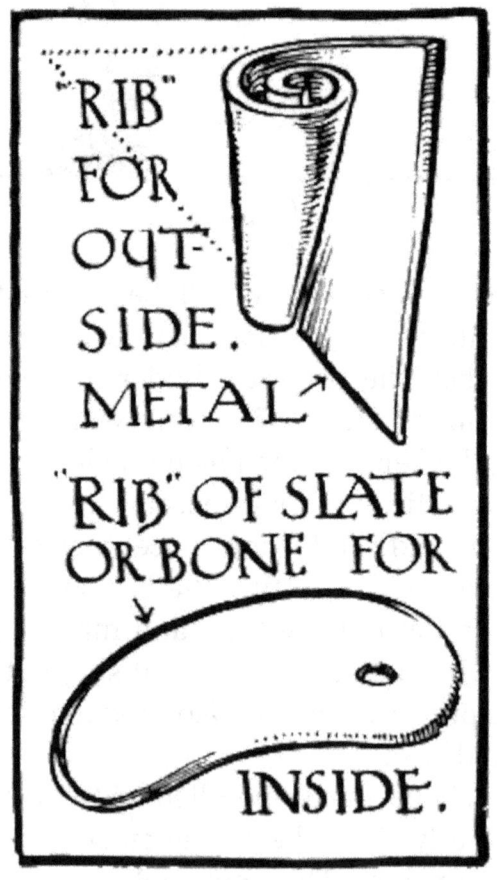

Fig. 30

The first primitive forms are far better left frankly for what they are. Afterwards when bigger and more finished shapes are attempted, they can be thinned and refined with the aid of the rib and a modeling tool, a considerable finish being put on before they are removed from the wheel. With bowls or large shapes it will be found impossible to lift them off without destroying the shape in some degree. For these wood or plaster discs will be required. The plaster bats need soaking in water before use and the wood must be three-ply to prevent warping. These discs are centered on and firmly stuck to a layer of clay run out on the wheel head, and when the pot is finished they are removed with it.

Fig. 31

Basics of ... Pottery

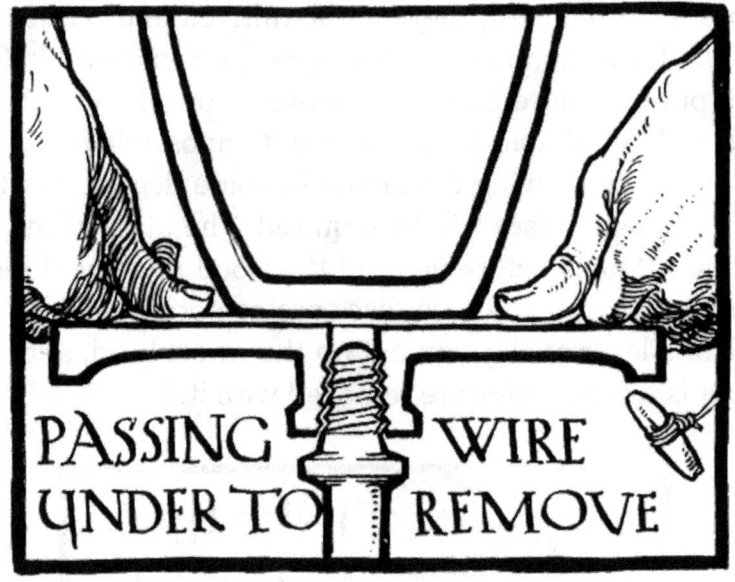

Fig. 32

All this sounds very simple, but the beginner will do well first to practice and master centering the ball. Until this be done, the rest of the work is worthless. After this must be practiced the pulling up, the pressing down, and the forming of truncated cones, then hollowing the ball and pulling up into a cylinder.

A true cylinder accomplished, it is easy to branch out into simple wide-mouthed vase forms. As the skill increases, shapes with double curves and long or narrow necks may eventually be achieved. Throwing to a set copy induces a necessary concentration at this stage, but once a mastery is attained, shapes seem to suggest themselves.

A small mirror placed so as to reflect the true form will be found of great service. When pairs or several duplicates are required, a drawing of the exact profile must be made and a "rib," of zinc or slate, filed to fit. Without such a guide the matching up is well-nigh impossible.

Fig. 33

When watching a clever thrower in a factory making some difficult and probably horrible vase, it is intensely interesting to see the fine forms evolved in the process. To the artist the impulse to stop him is almost irresistible. It was there that the old masters showed their wisdom and restraint. They stopped at the right moment and none of their shapes descend to the merely clever.

There is a nobility about a large vase lacking in a small one. Once the appetite be whetted for big pots the desire for size seems insatiable. The only way out, except for the born thrower, is the two- or three-piece vase.

The Chinese were masters of this as of every other process and we find that they frequently made vases of quite moderate size in two or three parts, sticking the pieces together with consummate skill. This process, however, should never be attempted until considerable proficiency has been gained in throwing to a drawing, for in any but expert hands it is doomed to failure. The shape must be carefully drawn out on paper and the sections marked off and then thrown exactly to size. Any deviation means

Basics of ... Pottery

endless trouble, with eventual disappointment.

For this difficult work the student unable to devote a lifetime to throwing will find a removable wheel head a necessity. Then a slotted one can be screwed on which will allow a plaster disc to be shipped back into exactly the same position, thus saving the difficult task of re-centering. For prolonged operations these plaster discs require to be shellacked to prevent the work leaving.

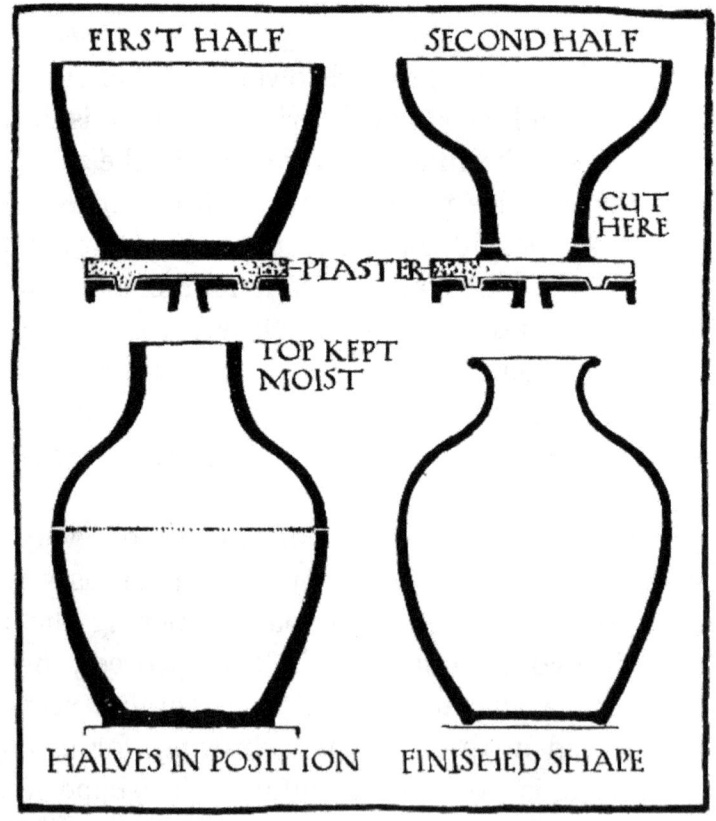

Fig. 34

George J. Cox

To start with a shape as shown in the illustration might be attempted. (Fig. 34.) The drawing made full size is hung in full view. Then the gauge is set to the exact width of the joint. The bottom half is first made, being cut square and true with the pricker. The drawing is reversed and the upper half thrown, the neck being at the bottom with a fair amount of waste beneath. When each part is trimmed accurately to measure, they are put aside to toughen.

The top portion will stiffen just as required, leaving the neck still moist. The bottom half will need watching to prevent the upper edge drying before the base gets firm enough to support the top when attached. A damp cloth lightly wrapped round it will help to insure the ideal condition for sticking up, which is a gradually diminishing state of toughness from the base up to lip, the junction of the parts being in exactly the same state.

When fit to handle, the top half is cut through at the lip, allowing a trifle for finishing off. Next the bottom half, still firmly fixed to the bat, is slotted back into its original position on the wheel. The flat surfaces that have to be applied and stuck are now very carefully and slightly roughened, then painted with thick slip made from the same body. These two wet edges are now applied and gently and firmly pressed into position, the wheel being slowly revolved to see if the two halves run true. When well together and apparently sticking, a little wedge of soft clay can be carefully run in all around the joint. This operation should be very thorough, and the clay wedge must be carefully welded into the sides of the joint. This is finished off on the outside with the rib and the inside very lightly smoothed with the fingers. During this process the top should be covered with a soft wet cloth, then when the joint has been made good and will stand the slight strain, the lip is finished off in the ordinary way. With three-pieced shapes the lip can be finished before sticking up, as the last part is thrown in its right position. If at any time the shape shows a disposition to leave the plaster bat, it should be stuck down with wet clay. The toughened shape can now be turned down in its upright position, cut off the bat, and the base hollowed in a chuck (see next chapter).

India. B.C. 2000

Basics of ... Pottery

CHAPTER VII
Turning or Shaving

"A sharp spear needs no polish."
—Zulu proverb

The turning or shaving operation takes place when the green shape has dried to a *leathery* condition. It consists in shaving the sides and hollowing the base until the thickness is uniform. The shape is thus made much lighter and rendered less liable to crack from unequal contraction. At the same time a fine finish is imparted to the surface.

One of the handiest tools for shaving is shown in Fig. 27, no. 6, but a piece of hoop iron bent at right angles and shaped with a file will serve. Small hollows can be finished with a modeling tool. An old piece of leather will close up and finish the surface. In factories a horizontal lathe is usually employed, the shape being fitted over a *chum* or *chuck*. Skilled men can turn shapes down until they are scarcely thicker than tin, but this, it is needless to add, is an abuse of method even with porcelain, and quite out of place with stoneware or earthenware. All that is necessary is to trim the thick sides, hollow the base, and smooth the surface. (Fig. 35.)

A simple way to arrive at this is to throw on the wheel a chuck of stiff clay to fit the shape, wide-mouthed ones being fitted over and ordinary shapes within the chuck. (Figs. 36 and 37.) A piece of soft linen is placed over this chuck to prevent sticking and the shape fitted and centered.

Basics of ... Pottery

Fig. 35

When spinning quite truly from right to left and steadied with the left hand, the tool should be gently applied as shown in the illustration. Hollow the base and then shave the sides, turning all down very gradually and improve the outline as much as possible in the process.

Care must be taken with the base. If it is not quite true it should be sandpapered to stand flat. A little experience will soon show when it is in the best state for shaving. If the clay is too soft, the tool jumps, forming ridges, or possibly cuts deeply into the form. If it is too dry, the surface crumbles and the pot is liable to break.

Fig. 36

Fig. 37

When turned in the right leathery condition, the shavings curl off like peel from an apple and all tool marks are easily removed. A beautiful finish may then be imparted with the leather.

To end the process the shape is reversed in the chuck. Those most important parts, the shoulders and lip, are carefully rounded with a piece of felt and polished with the leather. Properly attended to, this will save much work and disappointment later on. Then with all holes filled up, all ridges, bumps, and sharp edges removed, the shape is signed and put to dry.

For very delicate work in transparent glaze or underglaze painting, the whole surface may be gone over with very fine sandpaper and polished with the hand. This may be done provided the body is a fine one, for with a coarse body this is apt to leave the surface looking gritty. Some little practice will be necessary in throwing stiff chucks and centering the shape securely, but this once mastered, the method here described will be found to be expeditious and satisfactory for turning shapes.

A proper regard for process points to the desirability of leaving built shapes without a high finish.

Yet they also, if built carefully and stoutly, may be turned down in the above manner. The building up and turning down is somewhat tedious, but it is sometimes the only way by which a craftsman can obtain large shapes. A rather more simple process is to center the shape upon a whirler and turn down with a sharp wire tool, finishing off lightly with a sponge and soft leather.

To accomplish this satisfactorily the shape must be fairly soft, as there can be no quick spinning motion to enable the tool to cut cleanly as in the chuck or the wheel. When the head of the whirler is of plaster, it should be well soaked in water and the centered shape stuck down with soft clay. The hand holding the cutting wire tool must be held steady at a fixed distance from the centered shape and the pot may be sprayed with water blown through a diffuser from time to time, to keep it moist. Some clays will not, however, stand much re-wetting.

Fig. 38

It should not be necessary to caution the craftsman against angular profiles, splayed feet, or sharp moldings. Such features are foreign to good pottery, however suited to metal or stone.

With taste and judgment the irregular grooving caused by the tool can be made of high decorative value. In no case should the built shape try to masquerade as a thrown shape. When the whirler is used to shave down built shapes, they may be coiled very thick at the base, thus allowing more rapid work.

The attention must then be concentrated on the profile of the inside. In this way many shapes that splay out or curve boldly from the foot may be built, which would otherwise present many difficulties in coiling.

Basics of ... Pottery

CHAPTER VIII
Tile-Making

"VI thousand and fourscore of pavynge tiles delivered at Hampton Court, for to pave the Kinges new hall at XXVJs. VIIJd. the thousand."
 —Sixteenth Century memorandum

Tiles may be made of various kinds and sizes, but in every case they show an inclination to buckle in drying and firing. The larger the tile the stronger is this tendency to warp. The clay must not be so rich as that which is used for throwing and should be tempered to counteract the tendency to curl.

A tile box as shown in Fig. 39, or a variant of it, will be required for pressing tiles by hand; for plain tiles 5/8" deep, for others 1¼" deep, the size being calculated to allow for shrinking.

The sides hinge and the thumb screws keep it steady on the bench during work. For rough tiles, two strips nailed to the table will serve, the clay being rolled out between and cut in lengths as required.

For plain tiles the wedged and tempered clay is batted out into a slab a full 3/4" thick. The mold is dusted with French chalk, flint, or very finely sifted clay dust, to prevent sticking, and into it is pressed a piece cut to fit easily in the tile box, from the slab. This is firmly pressed into the box, considerable pressure being used. The surplus is scraped off and the top trued with an iron straight-edge. The knife can be run round the sides, then with the frame reversed a smart tap on the back will release the tile.

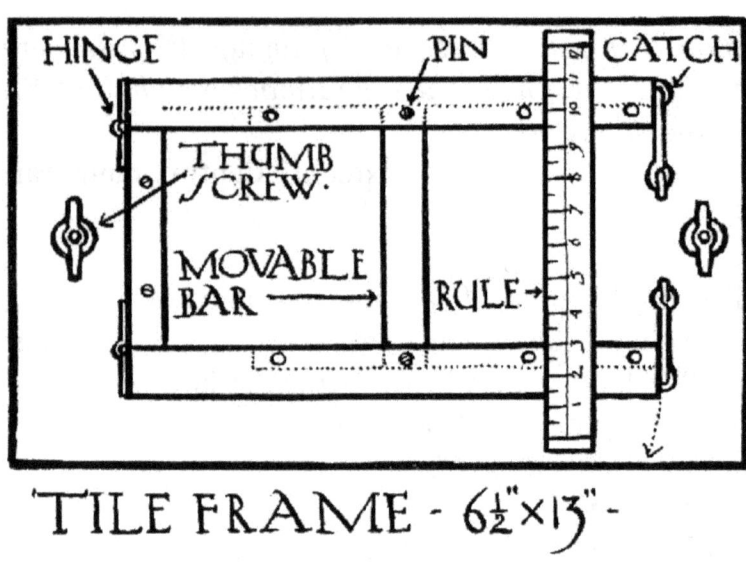

Fig. 39

Let the tiles toughen and then pile in stacks with flat pieces of clay or old tile between each corner and a true biscuit tile at bottom and the top. They can be piled one on the other with sand between or stacked like bricks with alternate holes for the air to circulate. This retards the drying, but in any case they must be dried slowly. With plain glazed tiles a little coarse dust sprinkled over the surface before the tile is removed from the box, and well pressed in, will give a slight interest to the surface and take away any mechanical look. If required for painting, the clay must be very finely sieved and the surface will need careful finishing by hand when dry. With coarse clay, a fine surface can be imparted with a flexible broad palette knife.

For raised outline tiles a frame 1¼" deep is required. This allows a plaster bat ⅝" thick to be placed at the bottom. The best way, perhaps, is to oil the frame and cast the bat in it, removing it when set and sandpapering the upper surface flat and true.

The design for the tile drawn the exact size on paper is now traced on this surface. It is far better to sketch it directly onto the slab, but this demands some proficiency if the surface is to be preserved. The design is then incised with a firm sharp point, clay squeezes being taken from time to time to show the progress of the work. The plaster should be wetted to insure easy working. At the finish the design should stand out in a fairly strong and deep line—square—not round or angular in section. (Fig. 40.) A chisel-pointed hard pencil will be found best for finishing. This gives a clear-cut line, not too round. The bat, sponged clean and porous, is then placed in the frame and the tile pressed as before.

Raised outline tiles can be even more satisfactorily made by means of outlining slip squeezed from a tube or tracer in the same manner that inscriptions are made on sugared cakes, but this requires much practice to obtain good results. When glazing, the colored glazes are applied to the different compartments with a brush.

As the glaze fuses to about one third of its bulk when dry, it should be applied very liberally.

It will be found that large or elaborate designs are to be avoided, as in this process they tend to become mechanical and look thin.

Basics of ... Pottery

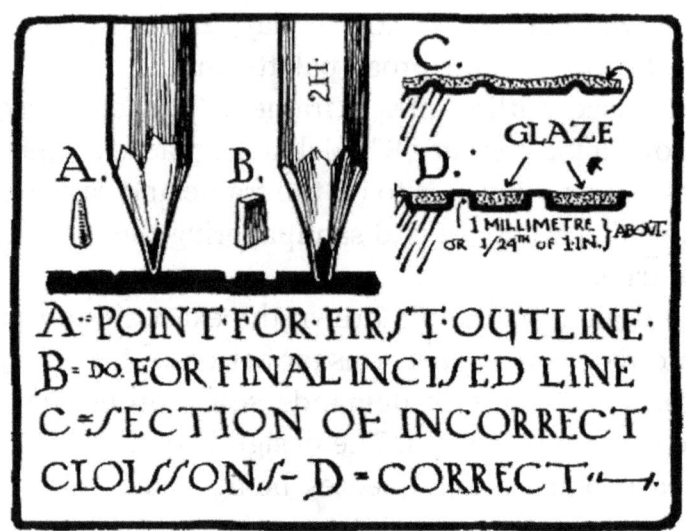

Fig. 40

The old Spanish and Moorish tiles in this style with jewel-like bits of color are excellent guides and might be studied with advantage.

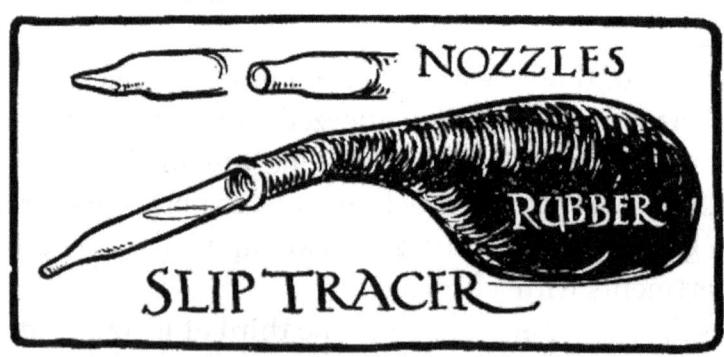

Fig. 41

The process of making encaustic tiles is a little more

complicated. Within the frame is placed a well-lathered or soaped plaster bat (or tile) high enough to allow only a thin layer of clay 1/8" thick being run out on top. On this when firm the design is traced or pounced. Then with a thin sharp blade it is cut down vertically to the plaster bat, and the clay removed until the whole design shows in white plaster beneath (see illustration 42). The face of the clay left must be preserved carefully, as it forms the surface of the subsequent press.

The bat with clay is now placed on the bottom of the frame to allow a cast 5/8" thick to be made. The plaster and the sides of the frame are slightly oiled and the plaster mixed and poured in. A soft hair brush will be useful to dislodge the air bubbles that are certain to hide in some of the many odd corners. When nearly set, the surface of the plaster can be scraped flat, and when set taken out of the frame and detached. The clay is picked out and the whole surface of the design cleaned and trimmed so that it will not hold or bind in pressing. This in turn is placed in the frame and a careful press taken.

The result is a sunk design into which a different colored clay is pressed, the tile being first allowed to toughen. The surface is lightly scraped flat and the tile slowly dried. When hard, the face is scraped again with a steel straight-edge, sandpapered, and dusted, when the design appears in two colors. (Fig. 43.)

The most effective clays are fairly siliceous reds, buffs, browns, and greys. When tempered with flint or quartz sand to a uniform degree, they offer a splendid opportunity for counterchange pattern.

If a soft clay that contracts considerably is inlaid in a

refractory clay, cracks will appear round the edges of the inlay.

Fig. 42

Thus it is found best to have the body of the tile made of the clay that contracts most. Where only a single tile is required a more direct method is possible. The tile is pressed and allowed to toughen slightly, the design being transferred as before.

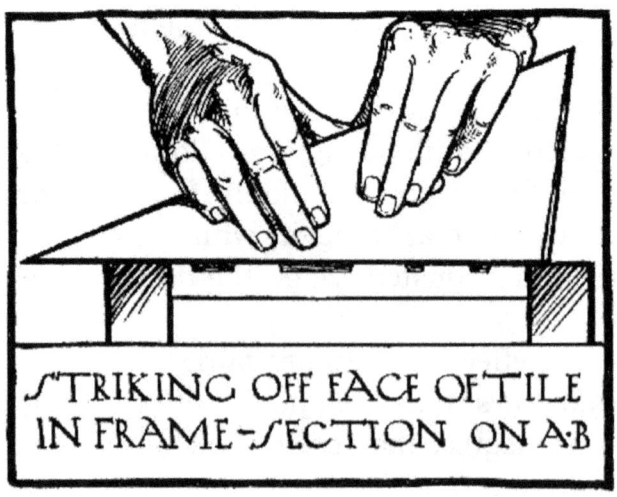

Fig. 43

George J. Cox

It is then cut round with a sharp knife and the waste removed with a wire tool. A certain facility of handling is required, for great care must be taken to preserve the edges and angles. This method is, however, productive of much fresh and vigorous work.

Encaustic tiles must necessarily be simple and bold in character, for anything complicated invites confusion; the best possible guides are the encaustic tiles of medieval times, especially the simple and spirited English and German Gothic.

The most satisfactory way to make modeled tiles or panels is to run out upon a stout board, cross battened to prevent warping, a flat slab of clay of the required thickness. Sketch in the design with a point and model straight away onto the clay. Care must be taken, if the panel is to be fired, to see that all the added work adheres firmly to the background. Where several presses are to be made, the edges of the modeled slab should be carefully trimmed with a bevel, the board oiled, and the mold made directly after the modeling is finished. The mold may be worked on in moderation. Lettering is much more easily incised in the mold than raised in the clay. For tiles needing much sharpness of detail almost the whole can be carved in the plaster. Unless done with great sympathy, however, this leads to a certain harshness and angularity that should be foreign to clay. Where a molded frame for a panel is required, a *strickle*, or profile, is cut in zinc. For short use one made from a thin slab of plaster will serve. The strickle is keyed to a straight-edge and dragged over the clay until the correct molding emerges. This is then cut into lengths and very carefully dried.

Basics of ... Pottery

The tendency of all transparent glassy glazes to pool in hollows and run off at high points must be borne in mind. With thick matt glazes any delicacy of detail is apt to be lost labor. These problems should be faced before the design is made, as in this process there is a certain quality of surface required by the glaze. On the other hand, in endeavoring to make a good surface for the glaze to enhance, it is easy to slip into the over-round and slimy treatment that characterizes so much modeled pottery.

Basics of ... Pottery

CHAPTER IX
Drying: Finishing

*"There nis no workeman whosoever he be
That can werke bothe welle and hastile."*
—"Merchants Tale"

Drying out is quite an important part of pot making. For this a drying cupboard is a necessity. It is easily erected, if the front and sides of wood be backed against a wall. Across the bottom, which should be open, run a row of gas jets protected above by perforated zinc or iron. At the top, which is boarded in, place a small sliding panel to insure a draught. With side brackets and removable shelves it should answer all purposes. A cupboard may be built over a radiator, but here the heat is not so easily regulated.

A thermometer inside the cupboard will be an advantage, for a wet pot straight from the wheel will warp in a warmth that would be quite suited to tough shapes. The green or damp wares should be put on the top shelves and brought nearer the heat as they dry. Large shapes put into the cupboard to dry quickly are very liable to crack across the base. Any flush of heat upon them through any aperture in the shelves will cause them to dry streakily. Turning then becomes difficult or impossible.

Bowls, if not too fragile, may with care be piled one within the other. This helps to retain their shape. Tiles are best stacked in piles dusted with flint or with a piece of clay at each corner between them. Tiles should never be placed in the cupboard until quite dry and straight. Flat platters or dishes require very careful drying to prevent buckling and should be reversed on a piece of sanded glass. When shapes are dried in the open air, they often get hard at the rim before the bottom stiffens. They need reversing to counteract this tendency.

To retard drying, which may often be necessary, a damp-box is needed. A large box, zinc-lined and fitted with plaster slabs, is an excellent device. The plaster must be kept moist with water. A well-tarred box with a close-fitting lid is more easily constructed and will serve most purposes. All work to be *stuck up* or modeled on should be kept in the damp-box until quite finished and then dried very gradually.

In all kinds of sticking up the body and the addition should be of the same consistency. Re-wetting is dangerous but may be resorted to in moderation with stout thrown shapes. Ornament added when the shape is nearly dry is very likely to leave in the biscuiting, although apparently quite firm in the green state.

Cast shapes dry very rapidly and should be finished before they become white dry. With practice handles, masks, and the like can be affixed in the dry state with slip, but it demands its careful and sparing use. Cracks or holes in dried shapes can with great care be filled, a stiff wedge of clay being firmly pressed in and welded to the slightly moistened sides of the crack. The plaster tools (Fig. 44) will be found very handy for working on the dry clay. With skill and patience much repairing may be done on unfired shapes, but it is a waste of time to attempt it unless the beauty of the piece warrants it. It is far better if the piece be faulty to throw it back into the bin at this stage. Once fired, it is likely to remain an irremediable eyesore.

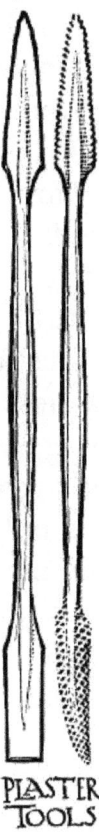

Fig. 44

One or two other points bearing on finish have been mentioned before in previous chapters, but these last touches are so important that they will bear some reiteration.

The finality burned in by the biscuiting should induce a careful and sound completion of each object; yet paradoxical as it may seem, the less finishing, the better for the piece. It is no part of a craftsman's work to go finnicking with file and sandpaper; too frequently nothing remains of what might have been a vigorous shape but a meticulous finish. The best Japanese work was superb in this respect and despite the many quaint and surprising shapes into which they fashioned the clay, it very rarely seems to lose its plastic character, it never assumes forms more suited to metal, wood, or stone. Again the character that comes with correct treatment is never smothered. Often the ribs or ridges made by the fingers or the tool in forming the shape are frankly left to contribute their quota to the general effect. The lips are rounded with scrupulous care and angles removed without a suggestion of weakness.

Where large utensils, ewers and the like, are in question, medieval pottery is rich in suggestion for handles, spouts, and such added forms. It is only when such additions are affixed that one realizes the nicety of adjustment required between the size, shape, and situation of the handle or spout and the vessel to which it is attached. It is here that an appreciation and an intelligent use of historic ornament is necessary.

Basics of ... Pottery

CHAPTER X
Firing Biscuit

"The Pope, the Cardinals, and the Princes of the World are astonished that such excellent and noble works can be made out of the earth."
—Eximenus. Fifteenth Century

When sufficient green shapes have been accumulated and are white dry, the next stage will be *biscuiting*. This process is the firing of the clay to a primrose or a white heat according to its fusibility. This permanently expels the water that is always present, even when dry, and converts the friable clay into a hard unalterable body. This may vary in color from the white of kaolin to ivory, grey, buff, red, or brown, according to the composition of the clay; it may be vitreous or porous; soft like common flower pots or so hard that it will spark when struck with steel.

The fire is the ultimate test of the pot and of the potter. It is indispensable to both. With but a small kiln the craftsman will begin to appreciate many things that can be learned only at the *fire hole*. Without a kiln he will not commence to be a potter.

The kinds of kilns usually found in schools are the gas and the oil kiln. The English gas kiln has an arrangement of nine or twelve burners beneath the muffle. (Fig. 45.) This is a fire-clay box, open at the front, set on fire bricks and cased round with fire tiles within an iron frame (see cut).

Basics of ... Pottery

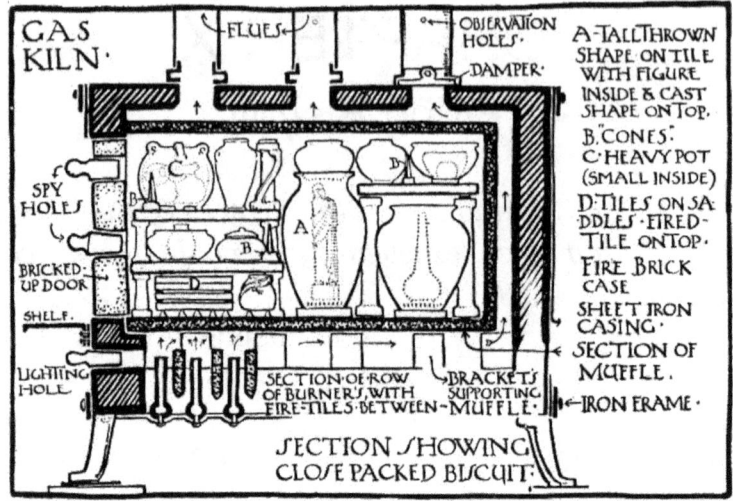

Fig. 45

There is an air space all round, except at the open end, leading to the flues on top which have dampers to regulate the draught. The open end may be closed by a hinged door or bricked up with fire tiles cut to fit. The defects of this kind of kiln are too sudden access of flame to the bottom of the muffle, causing it to split, and the impossibility of getting the front, where trials are usually placed, fired up equally with the back. An ideal muffle of this kind would be one with flues all round, gradual access of flame on all sides, spy holes each end, and the top to lift off, for placing. American kilns have flues in the door, and the chimney at the top is placed slightly forward, thus making it easy to fire the front up hard. They are usually fitted with two large burners, with air mixers, and a handy mica spy hole.

The oil kiln differs considerably from the gas kiln. The oil is fed through tubes into fire boxes some distance below the bottom of the muffle. It burns on asbestos fiber in an iron pan to which the draught can be admitted. The flames strike the bottom of the muffle and pass up through fire-clay pipes, which project into the muffle, then pass off through a twin flue regulated by dampers. With this kiln a long flue is necessary and any excess of carbon is liable to choke the pipes, and further it cannot be "sweated" up at the finish so easily as a gas kiln having a large number of burners.

It is a good plan when a coarse fire-clay muffle is used for glaze and biscuit to give the sides and top a sagger wash of lead and stone. This renders the muffle less liable to absorb glaze from the pots in glost firing. It also lessens the danger of small bits scaling off and sticking to the finished ware. The bottom should always be kept dusted with finely powdered flint. When cracks appear or joints open, they should be stopped with a pugging of fire clay and grog. A mixture of egg silica or water glass with fine grog and quartz sand will stop small cracks. *Siluma*, a fire-proof cement, with equal parts of sand, answers admirably for patching.

In biscuit firing the green shapes may be packed close together, with the lighter shapes on top of the stronger, but all must be ½" to ¾" away from the sides of the muffle. Triangular pieces of biscuit, called saddles, are used to raise the shapes off the bottom, but often a fired tile, sanded and placed on a spur or saddles, gives the best foundation. Where two layers are required, small props and fire bats, perforated to let the heat through, will be necessary. These form shelves as the exigencies of the packing dictate. (Fig. 47.)

For light shapes, thimbles and fired tiles will serve the purpose. (Fig. 48.) Where a shelf or prop rocks insecurely, a small wad of pugging (grog and clay) will give a steady bearing. Thrown bowls, if dried together and well fitting, may be fired together, and large thrown pots may be filled with little ones. Cast shapes can be placed on top of thrown ones, but no liberty is to be taken with them. Flint should be used liberally to prevent sticking, which may happen if the biscuit be over-fired. Tiles can be fired two together in tile boxes or stacked as dried. Flat ware fired in a small muffle requires very careful handling. Whenever possible, it should be placed in the center, on a flat flint-covered fire tile or bat.

One soon learns to pack a biscuit kiln, using saddles, spurs, stilts, thimbles, bits of tile or biscuit, and sand or flint as necessary. The thing that is a little difficult to realize at first is that built or thrown shapes, and still less tiles or modeled work, should not be hurried. Twelve hours is none too long to give to a 5/8" tile in the biscuit kiln. Although to all appearances thoroughly dry, the least hurry generates steam which will ruthlessly blow our best effects to bits. In packing, two cones or temperature indicators (Fig. 46) are placed somewhere near the middle in a position easily seen during the firing from the spy hole.

These cones are made of different compositions which melt at varying temperatures. Thus if the firing point of a body is known, a cone of that degree is used and the firing continued until the cone bends. This it does soon after it assumes the color of the surrounding muffle.

To eliminate the uncertainty that is likely to be present at the first few firings it is as well to use two or even three cones, one just above and one below the correct temperature. Placed in order there is little chance then of over- or under-firing unless so much sulfur gets into the kiln that the cones harden and refuse to turn. Calorites are sometimes used but are not so reliable. The cones may be sloped to insure bending to right or left, as a cone bending towards the spy is deceptive.

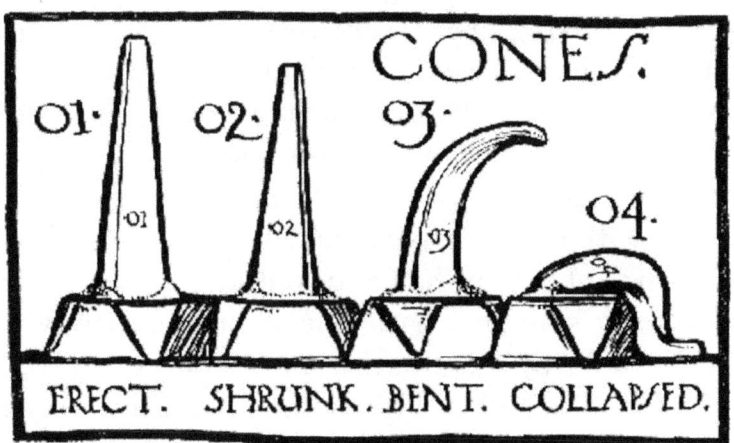

Fig. 46

A trial piece of biscuit being placed near the spy hole, the next thing is to close the muffle. In a kiln with hinged doors the spy hole is fixed and this fact has to be taken into account. But with a bricked-up door the spy and vent may be left where it is most convenient. These orifices have plugs that fit them loosely so that if necessary they can be pulled without disturbing the clamming. This clamming or stopping is a mixture of sand, sieved dust, ground pitchers, or other infusible siftings held together with a very little waste glaze and water. Where much is required, moist sand will suffice. This is plastered into the cracks that would otherwise let heat out of, or air into, the muffle, and so seals up the door. With hinged doors little stopping is required, except round the spy or vent. The crack above the door should not be clammed until the muffle begins to get warm. With this done and the two plugs out, all is now ready to light up.

With an English kiln, a good middle course is as follows: For cone .01, taking 12-14 hours. See that all the burner taps are off with the main cock on one third to one half. Take the reading of the meter. Pull the air regulators right back and the dampers out nearly half. Then take out the plug of the lighting hole and insert a taper. Turn on tap number 1. When lit, withdraw the taper and turn on tap number 2. Turn down to about one half and continue until every burner is lit, making sure that each one is burning freely with a yellow flame. With a kiln having twelve burners turn out all but numbers 3, 6, and 9. With these on one third, very gently push forward the air regulators until a roaring noise tells that air is being admitted to the Bunsen burners.

The flame at this time should be blue, and the stopper should be replaced. If the flame appears at all fierce, turn the taps down a little. If turned down too much, the gas lights back and will have to be turned out and relighted. The same thing happens when too much air is admitted. The burners require watching until the right pressure is known.

George J. Cox

Fig. 47

For biscuit of any thickness three hours on the three burners is not too much, the taps being gradually turned on to increase the length of the flame until at the end of the three hours the taps are at three fourths. At the end of the first half hour the bottom spy hole is plugged and when all steam has stopped issuing from the top vent, that is stopped also and the whole clammed, leaving just a small crack as vent. When three hours are up, the regulators are pulled back and all burners lit at half cock. Then all but 2, 5, 7, 9, and 11 are turned out. Starting at the half, they are gradually increased to three fourths in two hours. Then numbers 1, 2-4, 5-7, 8-10, 11 are lighted in the same way. Color will begin to show inside the muffle about the fifth or sixth hour, and the top dampers can come out a little, the front one more than the back, to draw the flame towards the door.

Basics of ... Pottery

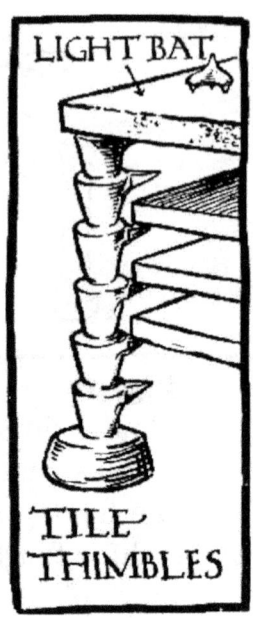

Fig. 48

When the eight burners have been on about one and one half hours the muffle will probably show a dull red inside and all danger of blowing will be passed. Two more burners at three fourths may now be put on and at the expiration of another one and one half hours the remaining two may be turned on. If the pressure weakens and the flame shortens, the main cock should be turned on. Just above the base of each chimney is a small hole and the flame should show through these towards the finish. If the flame flaps out of the chimney tops, it is so much waste and it should be checked at the taps. The dampers can come right out towards the end, being used to *sweat* the flame to the front if the back appears to come up too fast.

As white heat approaches, the cones should be observed occasionally. They turn the color of their surroundings when about to topple over and as the first begins to curl the trial near the spy can be hooked out quickly and tested. When the right cone is well down, the main cock and then the burner taps are turned off. The air regulators are now pulled back and after a few minutes the dampers are closed. The meter is then checked and entered in the firing book.

The kiln should be allowed to cool slowly for at least 12 hours, but the clamming at the top may come away and this will expedite the cooling without risk to the muffle. This time applies to a muffle of about 20" × 15" × 30" dimensions. A smaller kiln will fire up and cool in a shorter time.

Gas kilns as made in America vary in the arrangement of their burners, but the principle is the same. They are simple to manipulate and especially handy for firing "on" decoration, as they are fitted with shelves and uprights. The burners once alight, the flame is gradually increased, but where the pressure is uncertain, it is well to keep something in reserve.

Firing with oil is somewhat different. The asbestos fiber in the pans is well saturated with kerosene, the tanks filled, and the taps turned off. A light is applied to the burners and when both are burning freely the taps are turned on to allow a thin stream of oil to flow into the pans. From the merest trickle at first, the flow should be gradually increased as the heat develops. This is observed through the mica spy hole in the door and the one above tells when the flame is reaching its maximum. Should it flare over irregularly before the finish it means that the combustion is not perfect and there is danger of clogging. The supply of oil should be reduced and the draught regulated until the flame in the combustion chamber burns clear.

All soot or carbon forming in the fire box should be raked out and the oil supply checked, as it indicates a too liberal supply. As the oil in the tank subsides it should be refilled and the taps checked, as the increase in pressure is apt to vary the flow.

The later patterns of oil kilns have several advantages over the kiln described. The muffle construction and the burner arrangements are ingenious and practical, and need little manipulation to insure even distribution of heat.

The oil tanks and taps will need attention at each firing, otherwise sediment will collect and choke the even flow of paraffin oil or kerosene. With both gas or oil kilns the amount of fuel consumed should be recorded, together with the time, weather conditions, cones, and results of firing, in the "Kiln Log."

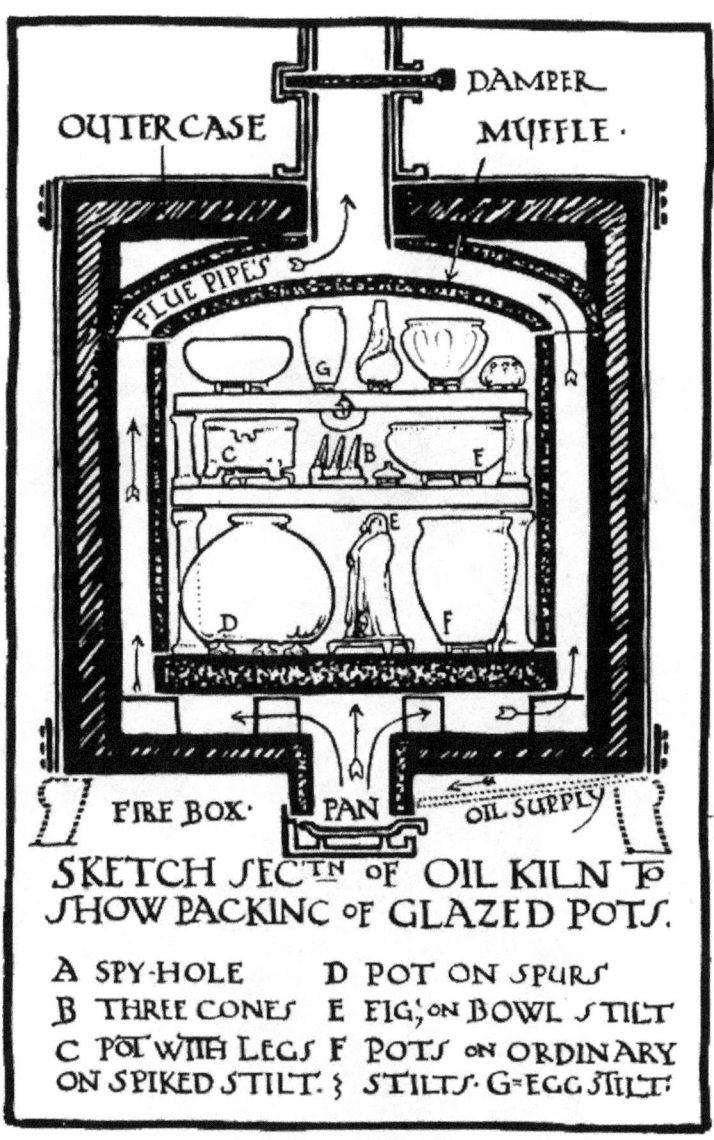

Fig. 49

Basics of ... Pottery

CHAPTER XI
Glost Firing

"When Fortune bringeth thee affliction, console thyself by remembering that one day thou must see prosperity, and another day difficulty."
—From El Koran

The hard porous biscuit shape will now need a coat of glaze and a subsequent glost fire.

Raw glazes for green shapes are now seldom used except for the coarser wares or peasant pottery. In commerce it is, however, largely used on tiles, moldings, and big sanitary appliances. For common cheap crockery a soft lead glaze, often galena, is generally used. It is applied with a brush, or the pot still leathery and tough is dipped in the glaze. Raw glazes have a strong inclination to leave in the firing. They are very difficult to manipulate unless they are of the simplest formula and fired very slowly. The addition of a little clay in the form of slip to the glaze will often counteract the tendency to leave the pot.

The ordinary glazes in dry powder form are mixed with water to the consistency of cream and passed with the aid of a stout brush through a phosphor bronze sieve into a large basin or tub. The sieves may range from eighty to two hundred mesh, according to the delicacy of the work. For ordinary work No. 100 suffices. The biscuit to receive the glaze should be quite clean and free from dust or dirt with the insides carefully dusted or blown out. Grease will stop absorption, but with opaque glazes discoloration is not of great importance. If the biscuit is hard and inclined to be non-porous, the glaze will need to be mixed fairly thick before it will cling; with soft and porous shapes a comparatively thin mixture will take readily.

No immutable law can be laid down for the exact thickness of the coat of glaze. All glazes vary. One sixteenth inch may be enough for one and far too thin for another. From one twentieth inch for thin transparent glaze to one eighth inch for matts is a fair average. It is well to err on the thick side to avoid an impoverished look. Trials on odd pieces of biscuit fired in horizontal and vertical positions will best settle the point.

In all cases the inside is first half filled with glaze which is rolled quickly round and out. The deposit is then tested with a knife. The glaze for the inside should be slightly thinner in composition than for the outside, as it is inclined to pool in the bottom if too thick. The outside and the neck are then scraped free of all splashes.

To glaze the outside of the pot the methods employed are painting, spraying, dipping, and pouring. In painting, two or three coats applied with a flat soft brush may be necessary. In spraying, the glaze is thinned considerably and blown through a vaporizer by means of a foot pump. (Fig. 51.) The shape, its mouth closed with a small bowl or saucer, is placed on a whirler in a draught box and slowly revolved.

The draught draws the waste spray away from the operator, who should wear a respirator. This method is excellent where any gradation is required. It is easily learned. Unfortunately, it requires expensive apparatus to render it safe with lead glazes. Unless it is done on a big scale and the waste glaze retained, it is also wasteful.

Fig. 50

In dipping, the pot is plunged right under in a tub of glaze which is kept well stirred to prevent the heavy constituents settling. (Figs. 52 and 53.) This requires considerable dexterity. In a school, glaze is seldom mixed in sufficient quantities to permit of this being acquired.

Perhaps the most satisfactory method is pouring. (Fig. 50.) The shape is reversed and stood upon a big stilt or two strips of wood over a bowl or tub. Then the glaze is poured from a jug round the edge of the base, until every part is covered. With a little practice a quite even coat can be thus applied.

Owing to the inversion of the shape it is slightly thicker at the shoulder and neck, an excellent point in glazing. When dry, the base is scraped and wiped clean with a sponge and the lip touched up with a brush.

Fig. 51

With matt glazes, as has been noted, a thick coat is necessary. If very porous, the shape may be soaked first in clean water to take some of the suction out of the biscuit. When glazed, it is essential that all dips and inequalities be removed. If thinly coated, the glaze will assume a glossy surface when fired.

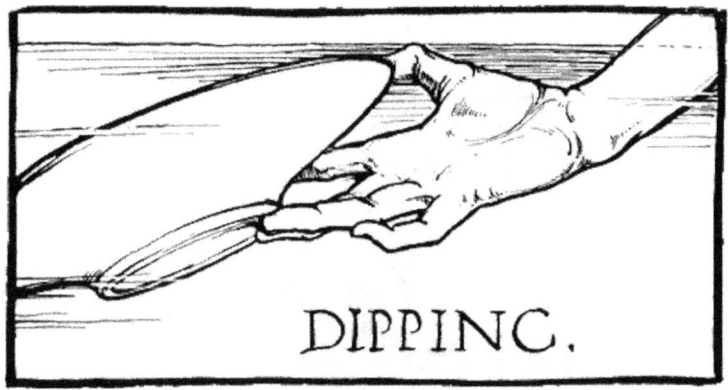

Fig. 52

Whatever process is used, the lip and base of a pot should receive careful attention, the rims especially should be thickly and evenly coated with glaze. The thickness can be tested with the point of a knife and any scratches or bare spots should be filled in and rubbed flat as they are apt to show at the finish if the glaze is at all refractory. Never starve the glaze, for a thin coat imparts a poor cheap look to any pot that is seldom remedied with entire success.

When only one kind of glaze is used, the application is quickly learned. With hard and soft, lead and leadless glazes, both opaque and transparent, and possibly a combination of spraying, painting, and pouring, the difficulties are greatly increased. Practical experience will be the only safe guide. But speaking generally, a sprayed coat can be thicker than a poured coat. Hard glazes give less trouble than soft if too liberally applied. Tin glazes will stand a lot of over-firing even when thin and the reverse holds good of matt glazes. Raw borax glazes require much more careful firing than raw lead glazes but often give better color results and are less liable to sulfuring.

Fig. 53

When glazing with a transparent glaze over under-glaze painting a thin coat is advisable. If it be thick and run, the painting is spoiled; but if, after firing, it appears thin, another light spray may be tried. But whole chapters of writing will never settle these points. Repeated trials on odd pieces of biscuit will elucidate more than many books. In packing a glost or glaze kiln stilts and spurs instead of saddles must be used to prevent the pots from sticking to the floor or shelves. (Figs. 49 and 54.) For the same reason the pots must not touch each other. With glazes requiring a high temperature the space between pots of different color should be considerable. An appreciable amount of glaze is liberated in the intense heat and a blue pot will often leave a distinct blue patch on any light pot placed too near. Soft glazes liable to run or drip should be placed on separate bats well flinted beneath. Any crack in the muffle should be well stopped and lime may be used to neutralize the effects of any sulfur that may enter.

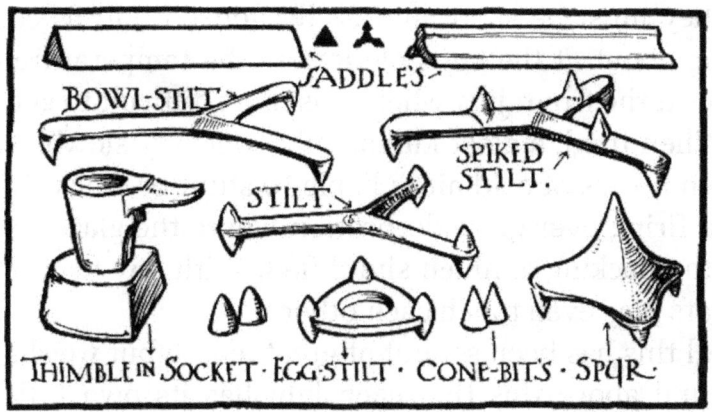

Fig. 54

As the back is usually hotter than the front the hard glazes should be packed first, and by selecting suitable shapes a good *setter* will pack a surprising amount into even a small kiln. The clamming should be done with care, as bits are liable to flake off and stick to the glaze. The top plug only need be left out and the lighting up proceeded with as before.

The gradual increase of heat is very essential in firing glaze, for any sudden jump or reduction will play all manner of games in a glost oven. The slow start is not so important, there being no risk of *blowing*. Indeed the glaze is best in a sharp quick fire.

Although cones should always be used and are excellent indicators, experience will soon show when a kiln is fired up. It may be advisable to go on a little after the cone is over until all looks fluxed so as to get rid of bubbles. These appear in some glazes until the last. They do not always go down on cooling, but those glazes that bubble through over-firing should be avoided. Possibly the trouble will arise from sulfur in the body which must be corrected. Trials are always useful but they must be small and easily hooked out, as constant poking about at the spy hole lowers the temperature of the muffle at the front, just where it is most difficult to get it up.

When fired, a glost kiln should cool very slowly, for any sudden access of cold air is liable to stunt or crack the pots. When firing over glaze decoration where the glaze does not run, the packing is much simplified. With low-firing lusters the pots may even touch each other.

All this has been set out at great length but we shall find over and above this that each kiln has its own little ways which must be studied and humoured before the best results can be obtained.

The chief thing to avoid is a sudden flush or jump in the heat. The main thing to aim at is a slow start steadily increasing to a sharp finish. The state of the muffle, a dry or a damp day, will modify each firing a little, but the above generalization will have a fairly wide application to the working of a small kiln.

   Unpacking is a compound of despair and delight, and is best done slowly. As the color dies the clamming, if any, may be knocked away, and later on the spy plugs removed. When comparatively cold, the door may be opened slightly, and left so for one or two hours. Then the front pots can be extracted but those at the back should be allowed another half hour. Be very careful of the razor edges of broken stilts or glaze dips. A steel chisel should be used for chopping rough edges or removing refractory stilts. If necessary the bases may be ground on an emery wheel until the pot stands true.

Basics of ... Pottery

CHAPTER XII
Glazes and Lusters

"I began to think that if I should discover how to make enamels I could make earthen vessels and other things very prettily, because God had gifted me with some knowledge of drawing."

—Palissy

It is in this department of potting, with its surprises, difficulties, and disappointments, its rare but exciting successes, that for most potters the greatest interest lies. To those of a scientific bent it is perhaps the summit of the craft, but the artist groping amidst formulas and methods may take heart. The finest work in pottery was not produced by scientists alone and does not depend altogether upon the quality of its paste, its unique color, or strange luster. The last word, the form, decoration, and craftsmanship, is with the artist.

It is beyond the scope of a book of this description to enter into a necessarily long and complicated account of the different processes concerned in the composition of glazes. It will be sufficient to indicate their leading characteristics plainly enough to enable the student to start experimenting. None can afford to miss opportunities for experiment, just as surely as none can afford to be always experimenting. For a full description of materials and glazes and their manufacture such books as those of Drs. Shaw, Furnival, and Hainbach are recommended.

Putting aside salt glaze we find a countless number of both lead and leadless glazes. They range from the thin silicious coating of the ancients up to the rich alkaline glazes of the Persians and Chinese; from the raw galena of peasant pottery to the rich Majolicas and fine hard glazes of modern commerce. Salt glaze is obtained by the vaporizing of salt inside the kiln at a great heat. The sodium oxide so formed combines with the silicates in the clay to form a very thin coat of refractory glass, intimately connected with the body. Porcelain glazes, though not differing so much in composition from the ordinary *fine* earthenware glazes, are extremely hard, being compounded of kaolin, feldspar, and quartz, with possibly limestone and ground sherds. It has in common with the salt glaze the close union with the body, so that when fractured the line of demarcation between glaze and body is indeterminable.

With a few minor exceptions the following list comprises the ingredients of all colorless glazes:

Kaolin
Quartz
Cornish stone
Feldspar
Fluorspar
Flint
Sand
Barytes
Bismuth
Gypsum
Limestone

Niter
Borax
Bone-ash
White lead
Red lead
Zinc oxide
Tin oxide
Salt
Soda
Potash

These materials must be free from all trace of iron. They are pulverized and some are calcined or oxidized. Then they are mixed in varying quantities to form the glaze mass. This mass is easily fusible when lead or borax is present in large proportions, more infusible or harder the more silica it contains, and very refractory if alumina is present in any quantity. The silica forming the glassy part of the glaze is stiffened by the presence of alumina, which stops any tendency to run.

Lead is very largely used as a powerful flux at low temperatures but is unsuited to hard glazes. Borax and boracic acid are important constituents of leadless glazes. They are used to replace some of the silica, than which they are more fusible. Matt or non-reflective glazes are opaque and less vitreous than the glassy glazes. They do not flux or run.

All these minerals are finely ground before mixing. Then those insoluble are mixed and *fritted*; that is, fused in a crucible or fritting furnace to a greater or less degree, according to the hardness of the glaze. If fused into a glass, the melted mass is poured into water to facilitate the next process, which is its reduction to a fine powder by re-grinding. Then the completing ingredients are added and the mass colored by the addition of metallic oxides. Of these the chief are:

Iron
Copper
Nickel
Antimony
Cobalt
Chrome
Manganese
Titanium

... and the more precious metals, in various forms, as oxides, carbonates, sulfates, and nitrates soluble in the glaze at great heat.

These metals impart the many varied colors found in pottery. Zinc oxide is used to brighten a glaze or to stabilize color. Tin oxide, which is insoluble at great heat but remains in suspension, gives opacity.

This is no more than a skeleton outline of the intricate processes often used in the fabrication of a glaze. The manifold minerals, metals, oxides, acids, and alkalis are used in a variety of ways by the modern chemical potter.

To all this seeming complication is added the question of pastes and bodies. There then arises the great problem of fitting one to the other. Salt glaze and porcelain excepted, the finished pot presents three strata. Outside is the glaze, next the body, then inside the glaze again. If the coefficient of expansion of these three layers differs, in other words, if the glaze does not fit, the result is *crazing*, that bugbear of the potter.

This crazing, which has been followed up and developed into their delightful *crackle* by the Chinese, may show itself at once or only after a lapse of months. It appears as a minute network of fine cracks over the entire surface of the pot. It is often not unsightly, but sooner or later it must cause devitrification. The glaze after a time assumes an evanescent iridescence followed by a dull smoky appearance; finally, perhaps not for many years, it decomposes and peels off.

With low-firing natural clays rich in silica and iron, the craze is not of much consequence. The body itself at a moderately high temperature becomes non-porous. With hard short bodies containing lime or chalk it may have quite disastrous consequences. Water placed inside will eventually percolate through leaving a network of grey lines all over the pot and completely spoiling its appearance.

It will be readily granted that, whether porous or non-porous, a craze is most undesirable on any piece of pottery that may be used for food or drink.

It is here that the commercial potter is such an admirable fellow. Many of the glazes on modern tablewares are perfect for their purposes. Sometimes only a little more fire is needed to stop the nuisance, but a bad craze usually needs more attention.

The glaze requires stiffening, and the addition of ground flint or quartz, China stone or clay and feldspar introduces alumina and silica and raises the fusing point. The substitution of borax for a portion of the silica can also be tried and will permit the use of slightly lower firing point.

If the glazes are bought ready mixed, the body must be altered instead. Refractory China clays should be replaced by more fusible clays or some reduction made in the amount of infusible materials. The addition of ground sherds or flint will have a contrary effect should the glaze peel or crack at the edges, as it may do on a very silicious body. In working with natural clays on a moderate scale it will be found best to mix "fat" or rich natural clays with those of a more porous or hard nature. A few graded mixtures submitted to a thorough trial should soon show when a sympathy has been established between the body and glaze.

The receipts given on pages 183 and 184 will make good colorless glazes without fritting if thoroughly ground in a mortar and passed through a sieve. Numbers 3 and 7, when calcined, will give much more even results and they can be colored by the addition of the oxides named. But simple as it sounds, the washing, grinding, fritting, re-grinding, and sieving is a long and laborious process demanding machinery, and on that account is unsuited to schools or potters of moderate means. Glazes like Nos. 1 and 2 will do quite well for elementary work but unless the appliances are to hand the manufactured article will have to be relied on for more finished and ambitious work.

If, indeed, you are already in possession of a good receipt for a fine color and glaze, one quite worth while, so much the better. Mix it and feel the joy of the Compleat Potter unafraid of spoiling his own good shapes with a faulty or unknown glaze.

Admittedly, to get anywhere in an original direction systematic research is essential. One must keep on experimenting, keep on hoping, and keep on taking notes; but at the start let us not be too impatient or independent if we wish to produce good pots.

There is often among young potters a false pride that prevents them using, and among old potters acknowledging the use of, the manufactured article. Why this should be is a little difficult to understand. A painter might far more reasonably be ashamed to use modern tube colors or a stained-glass craftsman as logically insist on making his own glass, as a potter in the Twentieth Century refuse to avail himself of the wonderful range of glazes that modern research has placed at his disposal. These resources should be used intelligently, not mechanically, or by the book—artistically, inventively, secretly, if you will, but they should be used—until the multitudinous experiments have borne fruit and repeated trials convince you that at last you possess some gem of research worth, as well it may be, the months of patient toil engendered in its production.

The various receipts are given on pages 183 and 184 without analysis of the composition of the paste or body to which they were applied. The first group have been used on common earthenware clays with complete satisfaction. They are to be considered as points of departure for future experiments in which they may be modified at will, and not regarded as a contribution to the science of glaze making.

In coloring it will be found that combinations of cobalt, iron, and copper oxides give an interesting range of simple blues or greens; iron and manganese browns; and so forth. The color mass or stain is ground fine and lawned, and from about 2 to 7 per cent mixed with the colorless glaze mass, according to the depth of color required. The ordinary under-glaze colors may be used to stain glazes, the percentage being fixed by small trials. For the rare colors—turquoise, crimson, or purple—a more complicated process is necessary and only perfected after many trials. The ingredients of these fine colors are naturally kept secret by their fortunate possessors.

It must be noted that a glaze suited to one body may peel or run off an unsuitable one. Then a colorant is affected differently by a lead or an alkaline base in the glaze. Again, copper and iron oxides may help to flux a glaze, whilst cobalt or nickel will exert a contrary effect. Cobalt, being a strong colorant, will need a sparing use, whereas a similar percentage of iron will merely tinge the glaze mass. And so *ad infinitum.*

It is self-evident that any attempt to emulate the vast range of the modern ceramic chemist is doomed to failure. To a craftsman the fabrication of one fine individual glaze or luster is an achievement of which he may be proud, and for which he will find abundant and varied uses. In this connection it is encouraging to the craftsman to learn from so high an authority as W. Burton, Esq., F.C.S., that it is impossible to obtain with purified oxides the fine tones got by the Orientals with impure materials. Further, that the simple glaze of the Persians—a mixture of clean white sand with soda or wood ash or potash—is still the best for under-glaze painting. Although tastes differ so widely, invariably it will be found that more and more heat will be the cry. Imperceptibly this leads to the desire for hard, cold, "fat" translucent glazes, neither matt nor glossy. And on the summit, far out of reach, stand the wonders of the Old Chinese.

George J. Cox

Lusters

There are several kinds of lusters, but the true lusters possess a pearly iridescence in addition to their color. The copper and silver *lusters* of the Eighteenth-Century Staffordshire potters were thin metallic films over the whole surface of the glaze. Gold or silver solutions were used. Only where the gold was fired on a white clay is there any iridescence, and then hardly so pronounced as to deserve the name of luster. The bismuth and other lusters made by the modern potter are combinations of metallic oxides and resinates dissolved in ethereal oils. These are painted on the glaze, transparent or opaque, but having almost invariably a lead base, and then fired at a dull-red heat. The medium disappears, and the metal in a finely divided state is deposited on the surface of the glaze. This, however, gives a painted look very different from the lovely irradiance of the Persian Hispano-Mooresque or Italian work.

With these the lusters were fired in a reducing atmosphere, one supercharged with combustible gases, the metals decomposed and fixed to the semifluxed glaze. The manipulation was not infallible and was attended with much risk; but the successful pieces are unrivalled, and according to Piccolpasso "paid in gold." De Morgan, who more nearly approached the works of the Italian masters than any other modern potter, used a very similar medium and method with his fine lusters. In the last few years lusters have been brought to such perfection, in preparation, application, and firing, that accident is practically eliminated. Glorious colors and gorgeous effects are obtained. Yet it may be said without senseless adulation of the merely medieval that nothing has been produced superior, or even akin in spirit, to the work sent out from Persia, Spain, or the bodega of the inimitable Maestro Georgio of Gubbio.

Lusters may be bought ready to apply. They are then painted on the glazed pot, which is re-fired at a dull-red heat in the ordinary oxidizing atmosphere. Once the painted look has been contrasted with the lustrous appearance of the *reduced* effects there is only one kind of luster for the artist. Fortunately, perhaps, their preparation is not easy, and the correct method of reducing is a difficulty to be overcome by practical experiment alone. Hainbach gives many practical receipts for lusters that are not beyond the scope of a craftsman. The reducing atmosphere can be obtained in an open kiln by the introduction at the right moment of any combustible giving smoke free from all traces of sulfur.

In firing with a muffle kiln the introduction of coal-gas free from sulfur is a matter attended with some risk at the necessarily low temperatures required by the lusters. It should be approached with caution, and each mixture will have a varied firing point, the correctness of which is established only by trials.

Lusters applied with skill and restraint enhance the most beautiful glaze, but in unskilled hands they inevitably vulgarize and cheapen. The fresh, unsophisticated renderings of the Persians or the Moors and the virility of the Italians should be studied, but not merely imitated before working in this medium.

George J. Cox

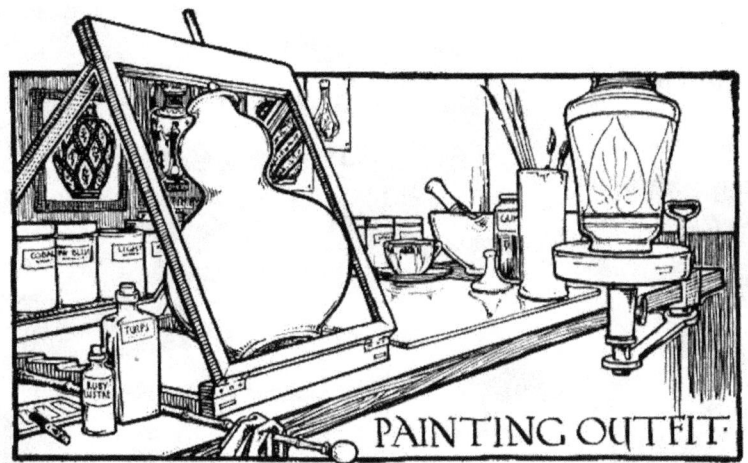

Fig. 55

Basics of ... Pottery

CHAPTER XIII
Decoration

"The world is still deceiv'd with ornament."
—*Merchant of Venice*

Decoration has been touched upon briefly in one or two of the preceding chapters. To attempt a description of the various kinds of decoration which it is possible to place on a pot, another book would be needed. Their name is legion. They range from the simple and entirely satisfactory work of primitive and peasant peoples to the wonderful enamel decorations of the Chinese. With such an enormous field and varied choice it is difficult to particularize and foolish to dogmatize. The hints below are intended but to stimulate interest in the at present unexplored fields that lie beyond the beaten track.

Any representative collection of ceramics will prove a veritable treasure house of suggestion to the student. All will be there. The difficulty is to choose, and choose aright. The bold brushwork of Cyprus foils the marvelous *familles* vert and rose of the Chinese, the faultless Wedgwood sets off the virile Toft. One sees how the Italians, with almost crude colors,—blue, green, red, yellow,—developed their wonderfully robust school of figure painters; then their fanciful *arabesques* are prolific of ideas. The Greek style— red and black and white—is a rich field waiting for the reaper. The peerless Persian pots, the plaques from Spain, the steins and stoves from Germany, the fresh Delft wares; these and many others crowd round for recognition and disconcert the choice.

But having come so far, let us not choose the horrific style that models most faithfully a cabbage, tops it with a lifelike snail as handle, and cunningly converts the whole into a vegetable dish!... (in S. K. M.). Nothing should be more distressing to the artist than to see great skill and craft thus misapplied. Yet how often does the search after false originality lead only to meretricious cleverness or vulgarity, which creeps in unseen during the too close struggle with the craft.

But our muttons need tending. Broadly speaking, all decoration falls under three heads: Glaze; Relief; Painting;—subdivided into many combinations of these three classes.

The application of glaze has already been described. A pot possessing a noble form and glaze is obviously in no need of *decoration*; no artist would attempt it. The Chinese and Japanese are safe guides here. Their rich glazes and fine forms are set off in the simplest and most effective manner. This is potting, pure and simple.

Under relief, we group all modeling,—raised or sunk, embossments, flutings, moldings, feet, handles, or applied figures. At one extreme come the earliest attempts at decoration in slip or clay, highly developed in the Gallo- and EgyptoRoman and Romano-British wares. The matured slip must be applied fairly thick to the still moist pot and then dried slowly. Any work applied to dry shapes is liable to crack in drying or leave in firing. Probably the most effective use of slip is seen in the old tygs and dishes of Toft and others of his time.

George J. Cox

The simple spotting and surfacing has been carried to perfection by the Martin Brothers, who have drawn largely upon the vegetable world for their inspiration. Roman Aretine ware shows finely executed reliefs of foliage and figures. The enrichment was probably worked on the original shape, a mold was then taken, and the vessel pressed. (See chapter on Casting.)

Wedgwood carried this method still further (too far, maybe) and used different colored bodies. The reliefs, so finely modeled by Flaxman, were fired, and from them molds of a very refractory clay were made, called *pitcher molds*. The reliefs were then pressed and affixed to the vase, and the whole touched up by a skilled craftsman. A naïve and unpretentious form of this decoration is seen in the stoneware and salt-glazed pottery of the Eighteenth-Century English potters and the jolly *Bellarmines* of earlier times. Small dies were used in the Orion ware, the pattern being stamped into the clay. German stoneware and the *Grés of Flanders* show sunk and relief patterns. Between the two extremes lies a rare choice of style.

This method of using patterns lends itself particularly to fine commercial work when used with the restraint seen in the best of the above-mentioned styles. To the craftsman it offers a welcome chance to enlarge his production, but he must be well equipped. It is easy to acquire the mere mechanism of commerce without its splendid technique. Finally, the further the relief is developed the less will be the appeal of form and the less the possibilities of glaze.

The next division is painting.

It is in this branch of ceramic decoration that the widest choice lies. The scale ascends from the simple earthy colorants applied to the unglazed pot in the manner of the American Indian up to the splendid enamels of China and the sumptuous but sterile wonders of—shall we say—Sèvres or Worcester. Much of the modern Eighteenth- and Nineteenth-Century work is such a technical *tour de force* that one hesitates to criticize it. But careful scrutiny will often show that the artistic difficulties have been undermined rather than overcome. Thus the frank frontal attack of the Persians on their absorbent ground or of the potters of Delft on their unfired tin glaze is never attempted, and probably never can be attempted in the factory of today.

The modern method of painting in fat oils on a prepared ground induces in any but the most accomplished a cramped and finicky style. The best and really most beautiful results are seen in the delicate *vertu* of the Eighteenth Century. Snuff boxes and ladies' knick-knacks exhibit the loveliest miniatures in an impressible medium. How far it is desirable to decorate pots with such pictures depends on the sophistry of the craftsman. (For, ever since painters were pampered by princes each erstwhile honest craftsman must needs try to turn painter!)

The Chinese who labored with infinite patience upon their pots still seemed to preserve a spirit lacking in the works of their western imitators, and their avoidance of realism saved them from the many pitfalls that yawned for the Occidental.

The manner in which the Persians and Dutch preserved their freshness has been noticed already, but the encountering and surmounting of similar difficulties is at the bottom of most successes. A few of the methods of painting pots are here set forth, with some odd variants.

George J. Cox

The colorants described under Glazes are also used for painting. Very finely ground and prepared, they are mixed with a flux or other vehicle and applied in various ways under or over the glaze. Simple colors can be made from the metallic oxides. They should be finely ground in a mortar well mixed with a little of the glaze with which they are to be used. This will do for the simplest work. For more subtle colors rather involved processes are necessary. The range of manufactured colors, both over- and under-glaze, is wide enough to suit all tastes, and when working on a small scale are infinitely to be preferred on the score of economy and dependability.

A method of painting entirely suited to beginners is as follows: A simple *palette* is prepared with the colors ground upon a slab of glass. The medium employed is a solution of gum arabic and water, the colors being applied directly to the green shape with a brush. The difficulty of firing glaze on the raw clay deters any attempt at high finish, and the absorbent ground develops a desirable freedom and directness of touch. When painted, the pot is dipped or poured in a transparent glaze and fired. The gum prevents the color shifting during the immersion, but does not prevent the glaze adhering. This method can be satisfactorily employed on biscuit. More finish can be obtained and a richer glaze used without risk. Much skill and practice will be required to produce good stuff, as each touch, although not apparent before, will stand out distinctly and often disagreeably after the fire. The gum must be used sparingly; any excess will cause peeling and prevent the adhesion of the glaze.

For a still higher finish the biscuit is sized with a

solution of gum tragacanth. This is smoothly applied until the pot is non-absorbent. The design, if elaborate, should be drawn upon the pot with a fine graphite pencil or, better still, India ink and brush. A common pencil is likely to show after firing, but the ink disappears entirely. The colors are then well ground and laid in with fat oil of turpentine or lavender oil.

To prepare the first oil, half fill a cup with pure turps, stand it in a saucer, and spill a little over the sides of the cup. After standing a little the fat oil is deposited in the saucer and the clear turps left in the cup. Long, flexible brushes holding plenty of color are used and the fat oil thinned if necessary with clear turps. The color should flow easily from the brush, being neither *tacky* nor too fluid, and constant retouching is to be avoided. Keep all free from dust. Heavy, greasy-looking masses should be scraped off and repainted, otherwise they will flake off.

When the painting is finished, the color is *hardened on*; that is, the gum and medium are fired off in the kiln, a dull-red heat being sufficient. This does anything but harden on, however, and the pot must be handled very carefully or the color will rub off. The glaze should now be gently sprayed on, and then the final fire is given.

Another way is to apply a very thin spray of glaze before hardening on, just sufficient to fix the color. The pot may then be dipped or poured without risk. In each case the oily medium must be quite dry before the hardening on takes place. After the glost fire the decoration is fixed and unalterable. Where possible, a hard transparent glaze is best for fine work. A soft glaze will always run if slightly over-fired, and the result is the obliteration of all brushwork.

Over-glaze decoration is applied in a very similar manner. Turpentine, fat oil, and lavender oil are used: the turps to run the color, the fat oil to stiffen, and the oil of lavender to retard the drying.

The color must be applied evenly and thinly, thick patches being likely to peel or crack. On hard glazes this process lends itself to elaborate effects. The hard and fast colors, the blues and greens, may be fired first, the delicate pinks and greys last. The whole effect may then be enriched with low-firing lusters. These, when bought in bottles, are ready to use and are applied directly with a fine brush, then fired at a dull-red heat. The pot should then be quite finished; quite frequently it is.

Pâte sur pâte or painting in relief colors is another process that has many attractive features. The colors have a clay carrier and are applied with a gum medium. Painted boldly with a certain amount of relief, this gives a rich enamel effect very suitable to simple figure decoration.

The full equipment of the painter will be as follows:
Colors, under- or over-glaze.
Brushes, tracers, and shaders.
A stick frame for holding the vase.
Turpentine and lavender oil.
A slab of ground glass.
A muller for grinding.
India ink and a color slab.
A palette knife of horn for very delicate colors.
Some soft rags.
Before risking decent shapes in the fire, trials,—on biscuit for under-glaze, on glaze for over-glaze,—should be made repeatedly.

Basics of ... Pottery

Graduated strips and stripes tartan fashion are the most useful and easily tabulated. To lay perfectly flat grounds some skill and practice are necessary. One method is to paint in the ornament or rather the space it will cover with thick molasses or black treacle. This is allowed to harden and the background color applied with a soft dabber. It must be ground fine with fat oil and applied very evenly. Then the tile or vase is soaked in water, which causes the treacle to peel off. The oil is allowed to dry and the piece fired. This fixes the background, and the decoration itself is next applied.

Pierced work if skillfully done is most attractive. The pattern may be incised on the "original," which is molded, the design then showing in relief. This again shows as a slightly engraved pattern on each cast form or shape. Then with the aid of a fine-pointed knife or plaster tool the pattern is cut out and the edges are softened to take away any metallic look. The Chinese and Persians are said to have used rice seeds in some of their translucent effects. The seeds were embedded in the moist clay to form a delicate tracery. When fired, the grains disappeared, leaving holes which were completely filled with glaze.

The decorative possibilities of simple incised lines and plain slip additions have been hinted at already. The slip may be colored red or brown with iron and manganese oxides or applied white to a colored body. Sharply incised lines may be filled in with color stiffened by the addition of a little *hard* clear glaze or China clay. Patterns may be dug out or stamped in and filled up with different colored clays and the whole glazed with a colored transparent glaze. Scraffito work is effective and not difficult. The green pot, tile, or dish is sprayed evenly with a different colored slip, usually red on white. The piece should not be quite dry and the coefficient of expansion between the two clays as near alike as possible. The decoration is then sketched in and the background or the ornament itself gently scratched away to show the ground beneath. It is then fired, glazed, and fired again. All these processes have their uses and abuses, but they do not lend themselves readily to elaboration or realism.

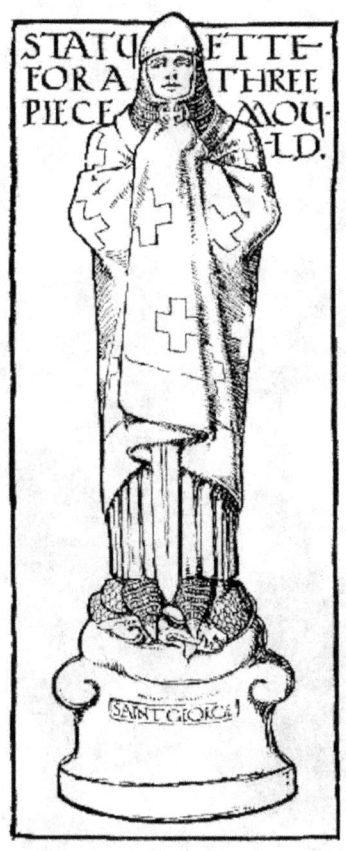

Fig. 56

Basics of ... Pottery

CHAPTER XIV
Figurines

"But if you carve in the marble what will break with a touch, or mold in the metal what a stain of rust or verdigris will spoil, it is your fault not mine."

—Ruskin

The making of small figures is an important department of ceramics scarcely mentioned so far. It is one offering exceptional opportunities to the advanced craftsman. In this branch of potting, even more than any other, the possibilities and limitations of the clay and glaze need close study if best results are to be obtained. The archaic Sung and Tang figures and the well-known Tanagras are far better guides to the beginner than the wonderful Dresden porcelain or the *bisque* groups of Sèvres. The Chinese and Japanese in their glazed figures show remarkable appreciation and utilization of the plastic and liquid qualities of their medium. Splendid and sound work, too, has been turned out in recent years in Germany and Austria, whilst the Copenhagen porcelain is world famous.

To start with, the simplest decorative figures might be attempted. Many of the little deities of ancient Egypt offer rich suggestions for two- or three-piece molds. Japanese Netsuke and Scandinavian bone carvings are other stimulating, if more remote, fields. Next, a more ambitious but still uncomplicated figure could be molded directly from the clay. As the difficulties of molding increase, the original clay may be first fired or a good plaster cast made. In firing the figure a very slow fire must be used, and the modeling must be done carefully, as free from holes as may be, and without an armature. Air holes are apt to blow, and additions of soft clay to the model when hard are likely to crack off in firing.

With a plaster *original* some retouching is possible before the final piece-mold is made. When modeling the head and face, the modifying effects of the glaze used must be realized, so that such detail as may be depicted shall have its full value in the finished figure. Too much realism in draperies with consequent under-cutting is to be avoided, and the inclination of all but the high-temperature glazes to leave prominent parts and pool in hollows must be heeded. Sharp edges are always bad, and projections that are liable to crack in the fire or break at a touch are a fruitful source of loss, and are, at the best, doubtful craft. It is quite possible to produce delightful figures glazed with low-firing glazes, and where a wide range of color is desired, they are the only glazes available. But for delicate modeling, where color is a secondary consideration and where refinements may be obscured by too much gloss, the grand feu porcelain or salt glaze are the best and only alternatives.

But each man to his taste. We will start with a simple *two-piece* mold for pressing. Small objects, not necessarily figures, may be modeled in the round, being designed therefore without under-cut to *pull* in two halves. They should be highly finished and then biscuited. The fired original is then shellacked or oiled and carefully bedded in clay up to the halfway line. If the figure be first dusted with French chalk, it will leave the clay without trouble.

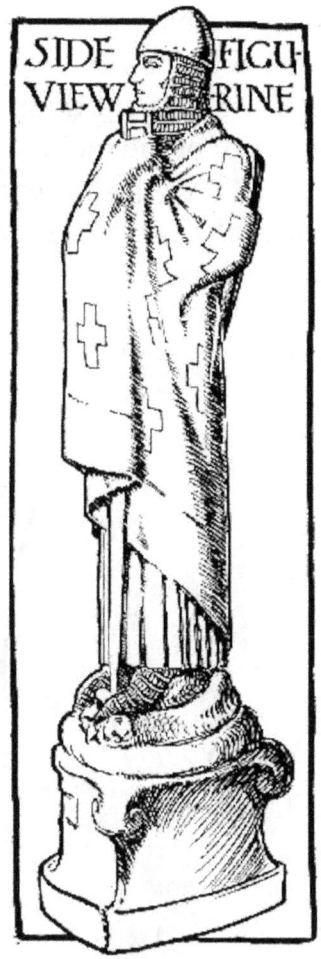

Fig. 57

Little walls being built, the first half is then cast. When set, the biscuit figure is removed, the sides of the mold trimmed, the joggles cut, and the figure fitted back. The sides are carefully clay washed or oiled and the second half of mold cast. When set, the two halves are gently pried apart and a groove hollowed out all round the inner edge of the mold. (Figs. 58 and 59.) This groove is for the reception of any surplus clay that would otherwise squeeze between the two parts of the mold and prevent their perfect adjustment. To make a *press*, each half of the mold is carefully filled with clay, well pressed in. Then they are applied and firmly squeezed together, until the two halves fit exactly. The press is then removed and trimmed up.

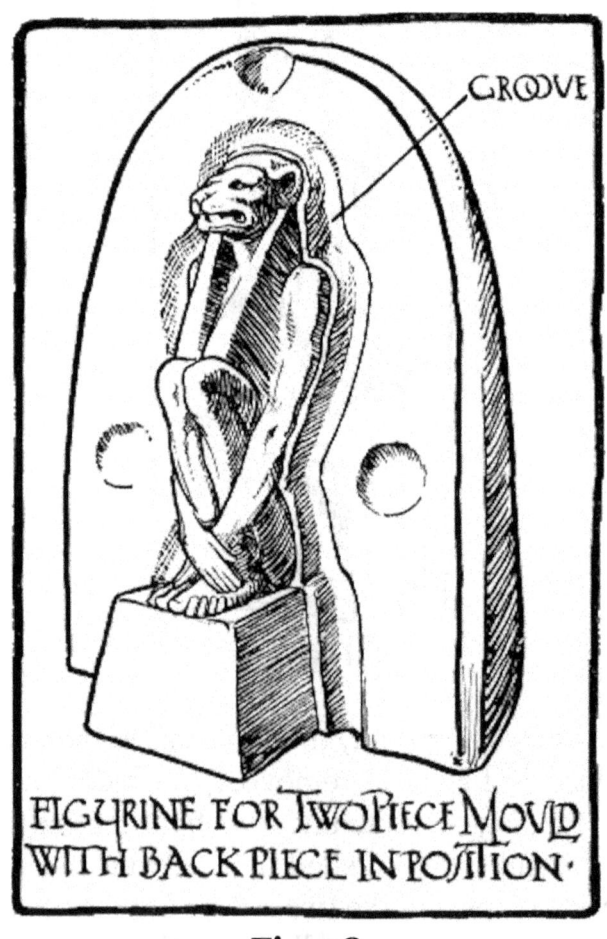

Fig. 58

The second essay might follow the lines of the statuette here illustrated for the three-piece mold.

A decorative treatment, giving stiff lines and a simple silhouette, is chosen. The hands are concealed, and the face, the only flesh showing, clearly cut out by the costume. The section shows the comparative depth of the folds in the drapery. Three pieces only were used for the mold, indicated by the illustration. (Fig. 63.)

In molding from plaster or biscuit the model must be absolutely non-absorbent and should be carefully treated with shellac, beeswax dissolved in turpentine, or parting. Beeswax is best for fine work and should be applied very thinly and repeatedly. Clay originals need no preliminary treatment, if the clay is still plastic.

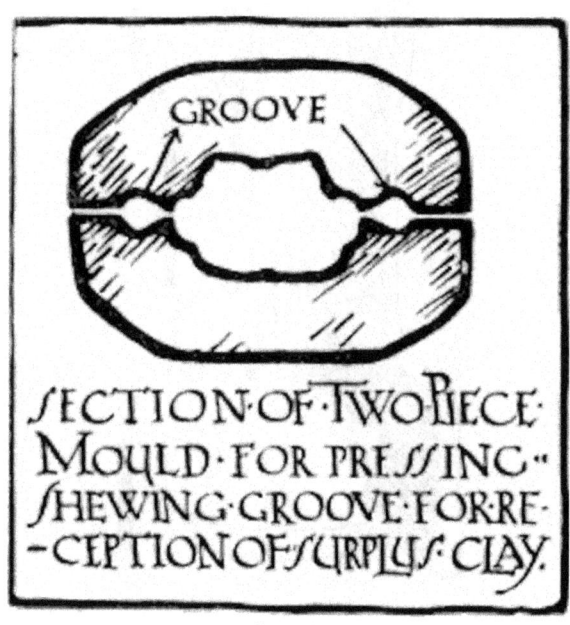

Fig. 59

The divisions of the mold being decided upon, plastic clay is rolled out thin, cut into strips, and built round the section, as shown in the illustrations. (Figs. 60 and 61.) The exposed figure within the clay walls is then very slightly filmed with olive oil. The plaster is then mixed and thrown on or poured. The walls should stand out at right angles to the circumference of the figure or so nearly as the exigencies of the figure permit. They should be buttressed where needing support, and be deep enough to give a good thickness to the mold.

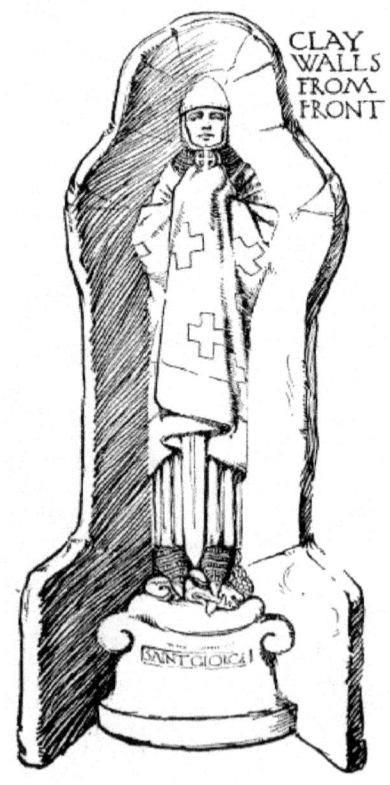

Fig. 60

When the plaster sets, they may be removed, and when quite hard, the plaster itself detached. This comes away quite readily from the clay, but is apt to hold on plaster or biscuit. A little water dropped from a clean sponge onto the cleaving line will often release the two parts.

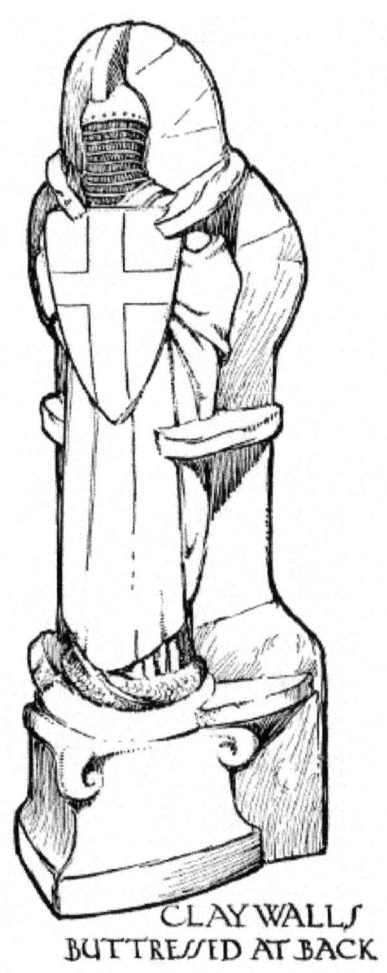

Fig. 61

Basics of ... Pottery

The model is cleaned up and the sides of the first section trimmed, slight joggles made where they will not bind, and the edges carefully shellacked or claywashed. (Fig. 62.) Model and section are then fitted together and the next section made in a similar manner, except that only one wall of clay will be built. The second section is treated in the same way, and for the last piece the clay wall is unnecessary, the plaster being poured directly in between the two other sections. Where the plaster has to be sprinkled on, or there is any danger from splashes, the exposed parts of the model should be protected with soft paper.

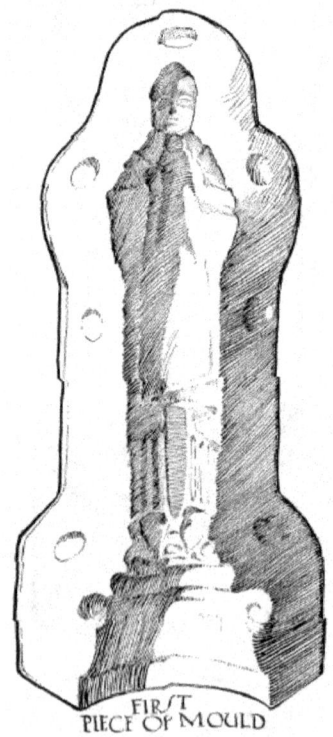

Fig. 62

The last piece being set, the original is removed, the mold assembled, trimmed, or fettled, tied up, and set to dry. The casting, or pressing if it be large enough, is proceeded with as before described, the slip being poured in at the base. When removed from the mold, the open base of the cast may be closed with a thin slab of clay slip poured on to a plaster bat and allowed to set for that purpose. When tough, the figure should be touched up with skill and reticence. Finally, a little hole is made in the closed base and another as inconspicuously as may be in the back of the head, to prevent blowing in the fire.

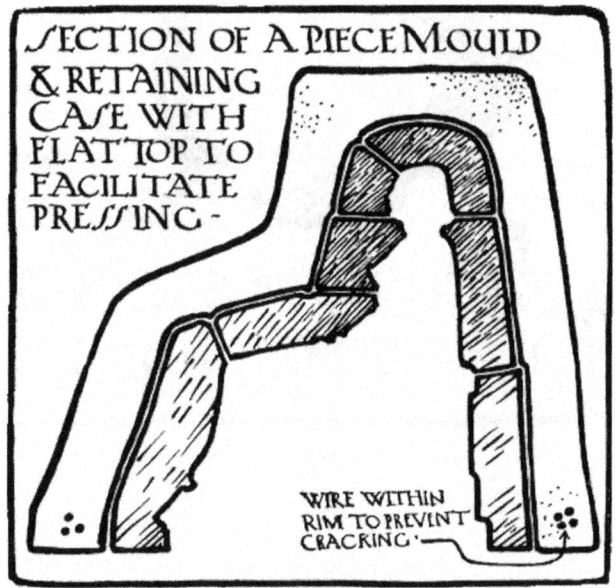

Fig. 63

With more complex figures many more pieces will be needed for the mold. They are made in the same way, but

Basics of ... Pottery

are carefully trimmed and then encased in an outer frame or jacket of plaster. (Fig. 63.) Large figures should be pressed; the head first, the different sections of the mold being fitted into the containing case as the work progresses. More retouching is needed with pressed figures, but the time spent is well spent, for they possess a substance, and when retouched with art, a character, that is lacking in the more fragile cast.

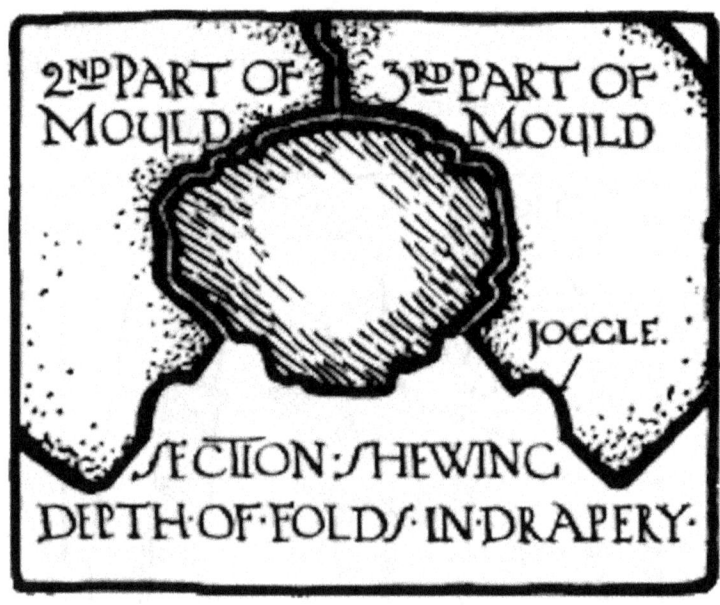

Fig. 64

Fig. 65
Early Greek Kiln.

Basics of ... Pottery

CHAPTER XV
Kilns

"By many long, laborious, and chargeable experiments he hath found out."
—Extract from an old potter's patent

What must be the first representation of a kill, or kiln, is found at Beni Hassan. It appears to be square in form, and the potter is shown feeding the fire at the base. In the same illustration he is depicted unpacking or drawing the ware from the top. The cut from the Greek Hydra gives a very similar kiln, but a vessel in the museum of Berlin shows one with a beehive shape.

The kilns left scattered about Europe by the Romans were usually of this domed kind, circular in plan, with one fire hole. The floor of the kiln was of pierced slabs, and the flames issuing thence enveloped the ware piled within and escaped through a vent in the top. The packing and firing is described in *Ceramic Art in Great Britain*, by L. Jewitt, F.S.A. It fully explains the trepidation of the old potters, who, before each firing, were wont to consult the moon and stars and evoke the aid of the gods. This is happily set forth in Cowper's translation of one of Homer's epigrams, wherein he expresses the pious hope that if the false potter "stoops to peep into his furnace, may the fire flash in his face and scorch it"; a risk often faced by potters, false or true!

The smothering, or reducing, as then practiced, was

similar to the *lustering* methods used in Italy in the Sixteenth Century, or in the manufacture of the *blue* bricks today. The Japanese and Chinese built small kilns in tiers on the side of a hill. Starting with the lowest, the waste heat was utilized to warm up the kiln above, thus saving time and fuel. The Chinese used heavy saggars, and specimens of these with portions of melted pots still adhering to them attest the enormous heats to which they frequently attained.

Modern kilns subdivide roughly into biscuit, glost, and enamel. The first is used for firing the green or clay shapes, the second for the hard fire of the glazed ware, and the last-named for fixing on the added decoration. Sometimes a kiln is used for the double function of biscuiting and glazing.

Of modern kilns the one still most widely used approximates to the bottle-shaped, simple, up-draught kiln. It contains one or two chambers with hatch for entry, flue or chimney, and anything from three to nine fire holes. The section of such a kiln is here shown and represents a fair average up-draught kiln (Fig. 66), variants of which type are working in most pottery districts today. In these kilns the flames rush in at the fire holes, play on the built-up *bungs* of saggars, and escape through the top vent.

In a two chamber kiln, as sometimes used for porcelain, the glaze is put in the lower chamber to receive the hottest fire, the biscuit in the upper getting a gentle fire. Where the fire enters directly into the kiln in any large volume, *bags* or small chimneys are built up inside the mouths to save the saggars from the worst of the fire.

Of late the single-chamber, down-draught kiln has come into favor, as it is easily packed and economical of heat. Bags of firebrick protect the saggars from the roughest fire and direct the flames to the crown of the chamber, from which point they descend to pass out through flues in the floor of the kiln. (Fig. 67.) Biscuit ovens are often of this type, either domed or flat arched.

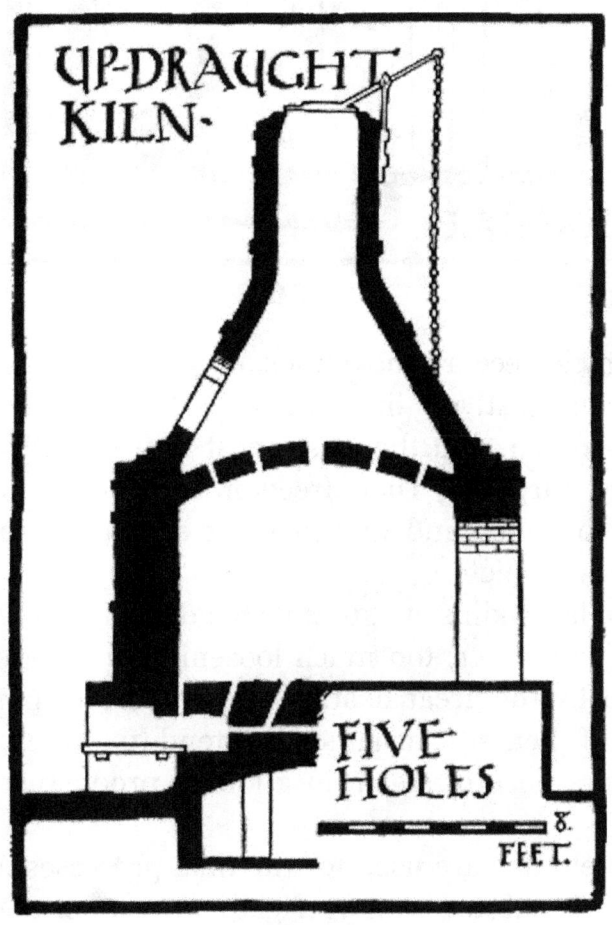

Fig. 66

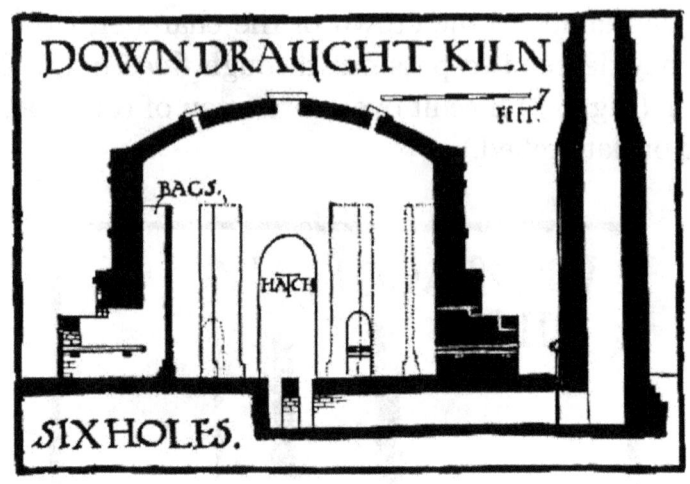

Fig. 67

The most recent innovations are gas and oil kilns. They require comparatively little manual labor in the firing, are easily regulated, and the waste heat is frequently used for secondary purposes. Their freedom from smoke and their economy of labor and money must eventually render the other types obsolete.

These large kilns are strongly banded with iron supports designed to prevent too much loosening of the walls when expanded by the great heat. A very important point is the draining of their site, as large kilns tend to attract moisture, and the presence of steam in a kiln is productive of much damage.

Enamel kilns are used for the final processes where the glazed pot is painted with over-glaze or enamel colors. They are of no great size and are made of fire-clay slabs or even iron plates when the enamel is soft. The flames play all round the muffle or fire-clay box during the firing, but no flame or fume is allowed access to the inside. (Fig. 68.)

In packing a kiln with biscuit or glaze much care, thought, and expedition have to be exercised. An experienced setter is essential in a factory if the pots are to have every chance in the fire, for all kilns vary and have their hot and *cool* corners. First, the floor is well bedded with quartz sand or flint that will not vitrify but will provide a good setting for the bottom saggars. These saggars are fire-clay *boxes*, round or oval, rarely square, and without lids, in which the pots are placed. Piled one above another they form the *bungs*, the bottom of one supplying the top of that beneath. These bungs are built at intervals that permit the flames to penetrate between them and give a good even fire all over the chamber.

Fig. 68

In actual practice some parts of a kiln are hotter than others, and it is here that a good setter shows his capabilities, setting the thin wares in the softest places and putting the heavier biscuit or hard glaze in the hottest corners. With biscuit the setting is not difficult except where delicate or friable ware may need very careful bedding and propping. With clean saggars the biscuit may touch the sides, and a competent man will pile an enormous amount of biscuit into a kiln without risk. In the glost kiln the ware requires gentle handling and must touch nothing but the spur or support. The saggars are usually given a saggar wash of lead and stone to prevent them absorbing glaze from the wares, for a glazed pot placed too near a raw saggar is very likely to come out with a thin or dry patch.

When the pot is firmly placed on its stilt, a roll of *pugging* is placed round the rim of the saggar; this provides a firm bed for the next above it and also stops the entry of dust and flame. This pugging is made from clay or marl mixed with ground sherds, sieved gravel, or some non-vitreous dust to prevent it sticking to the saggars. The plugging is made malleable with a little water and rolled out by hand or pressed through a die. It will readily be seen that a carelessly built bung of any height may slip in the stress of firing, and its fall would most likely involve others, whilst any slight movement may be sufficient to cause a vase to topple off its stilt. In a down-draught kiln the bungs over any vent must be raised on fire tiles to permit the escape of the flames. When all the bungs are filled up and piled in position, the trials and cones placed, the hatch is bricked up. Spy holes are left where necessary, and the whole well clammed to prevent the loss of heat during firing. When fired, the hatch may be very gradually loosened to accelerate the cooling.

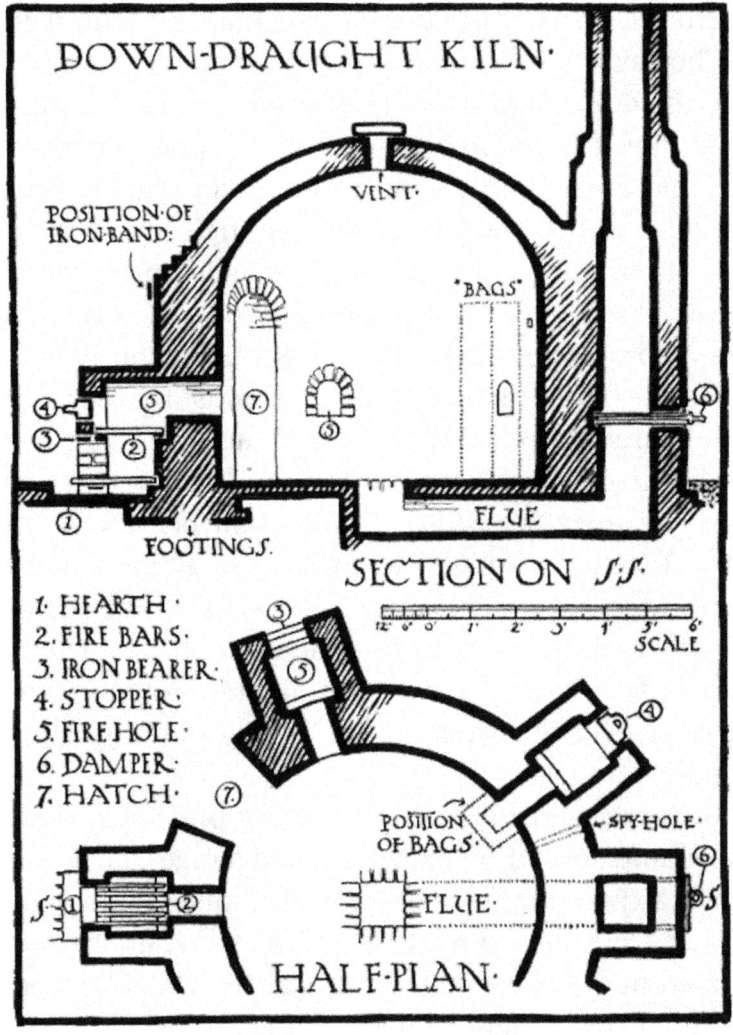

Fig. 69

The fireman's job is one of the most arduous and

important of all the prolonged processes of potting. Coming as it does at the end, it may make or mar kilns of great value, and it requires more than ordinary judgment and nerve. The chief troubles arise from bad or irregular draught or impure fuel. They express themselves in the form of clinkered holes, excessive smoke, and irregularly fired or sulfured ware. The term *sulfured* is applied to pots that come out gloomy or dulled and is said to be equally due to a reducing fire or an oxidizing one. In the former an insufficiency of air causes excess of carbon in the kiln and the absorption of oxygen from the glaze. In the latter an excess of air (oxygen) allows sulfur vapor, if present, to attach itself to the glaze.

The fire bars, fire holes, and flues must be kept clear and the fuel carefully selected if these things are to be avoided. The aim, as previously stated, is a gradually increasing fire, sharper towards the finish. For this purpose some potters finish off with wood which gives a long flame free from sulfur and clears the glaze. Even when sulfured, a clear flame at the finish will remove many ill effects. The baiting should be fairly heavy at the start, lighter and more frequent towards the finish, when smoke in any quantity should be avoided.

For temperature gauges, the cones previously described are used and should be placed in an average place, screened as much as possible from draught or flame. Small sight pots and glaze rings placed near the spies can be hooked out and examined and are valuable aids, but their exposed position and the corrosive action of the flames must be taken into account. Pyrometers are also used, but with all these aids the experienced fireman pays due regard to sight and color.

For a craftsman, the kilns that have been described are

unsuitable on account of their size, if they are not altogether beyond his means. But a kiln of some sort is indispensable to a potter. The craftsman is nothing if not inventive. Small trials can be fired in crucibles in an open fire or on a gas ring. I have heard of some preliminary success with a gas cooker, discounted later by a frontal attack from the cook. Considerable knowledge can be gained from small, easily constructed, experimental kilns.

The small trial kiln shown (Fig. 70) was constructed with a stout old *crock*, over which was built a core of bricks plastered with marl. The fire was started at each corner at the bottom, and when well alight, fed from the top with coke. A small spy at one corner closed with a piece of biscuit gave some idea of the progress of the firing. This, of course, had to be practically rebuilt at each firing, but as a makeshift was quite satisfactory.

Fig. 70

Basics of ... Pottery

Fig. 70a

The gas and oil kilns described in Chapter IX are excellent as far as they go, and indeed the only practicable kind for indoor schools. But their restricted size soon becomes irksome to a craftsman, whilst the expense of firing makes only the finest work remunerative. For over-glaze work they are excellent, but for some reason glazes fired in them seem to lack some of the richness and maturity the same glazes exhibit when fired in the slower and more soaking fire of a brick kiln. The dug-out kiln here depicted (Fig. 71) would be quite suitable for summer schools or for a craftsman making soft peasant pottery. The section and sketch will indicate its construction. The materials are hard bricks and stout old boiler plates, or sheet iron. To pack or unpack, the middle section of the roof would have to be removed each time, and all glazed pots would need protection from scalings and gravel from above. The roof will sag at any big heat, and if of thin iron, will need propping. The firing would be done with soft coal or wood; a very slow start, with a brisk draught and a long flame at the finish.

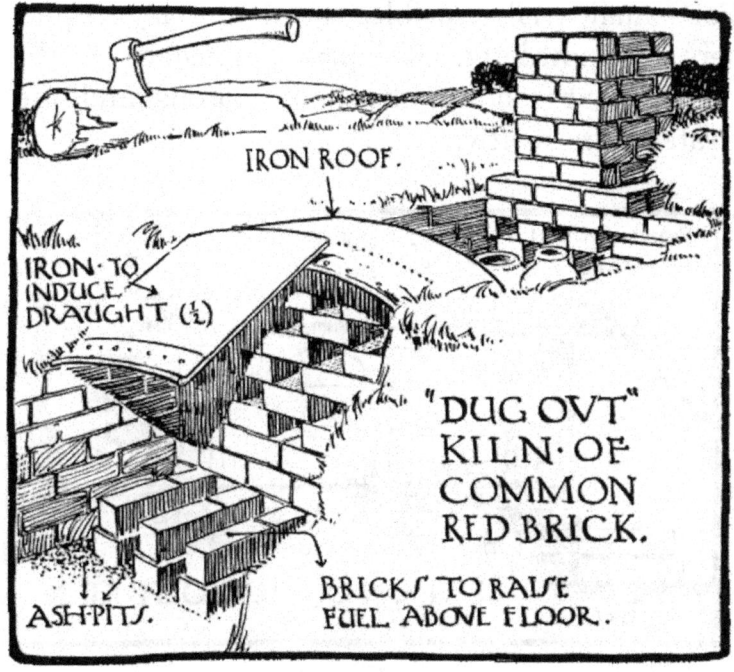

Fig. 71

Of course the front will be hotter than the back, but if saggars can be obtained, the glaze may be placed in them to the front with the biscuit protected behind. Clay shapes fired up at the front may bend towards the fire, and any broken crocks should be used to screen them.

The making of rough saggars is not difficult if a supply of fire clay is to hand, or clay and grog will serve at a pinch. The clay is rolled out and the saggar stuck up, much as described on page 32.

Every joint must be carefully welded and the whole thoroughly dried. Then they are fired up in the kiln, *very* gently at first, and carried up to a temperature considerably above that which they will be subjected to when in use.

For small trial crucibles ordinary clay mixed with pitchers and powdered coke proves satisfactory; the coke when fired out renders the body porous and the heat penetrates more swiftly.

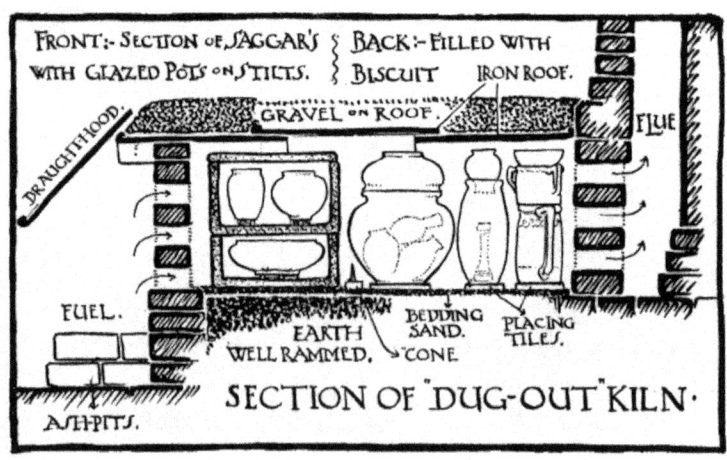

Fig. 71a

To construct the muffle kiln shown at Fig. 72 the aid of a competent bricklayer would probably be required. In this kiln glaze and biscuit would fire up without saggars, but will take rather longer. The plan and elevation of this particular kiln are given with all reserve. The design would probably require considerable adjustment and modification before complete satisfaction was obtained.

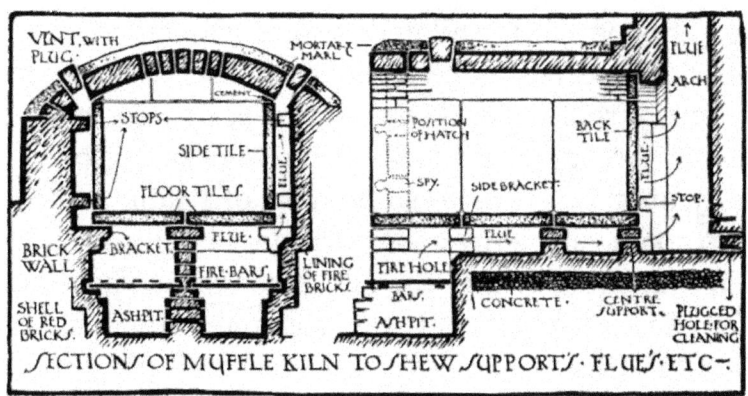

Fig. 72

A down-draught kiln, although more difficult to construct than an up-draught, is more economical in the end and does its work more evenly. For the benefit of those that may like to build a small and moderately cheap kiln drawings are here given. This kiln was built by me when I had very little practical experience of kilns other than gas, but it served its purpose well. It was not banded, but this is essential if the kiln is to stand hard and frequent fire. Firebricks were used for the fireholes, flues, floor, core, and dome; strong stock bricks for the rest.

The glazed ware, which was fired harder than the biscuit, was saggared in bungs as usual up to about five feet; the biscuit piled on top and protected by old saggars and cracked pots from the roughest fire. There were no bags in this kiln, but the saggars used were very strong and had stood a much greater heat than that to which they were subjected in this kiln, so that they showed very little wear or tear after twenty firings. The stack of sixteen feet gave a good sharp draught, increased if necessary by the addition of an iron chimney and regulated by an iron damper.

A wind screen or *hovel* is advisable for rough nights, and some sort of roof is necessary to protect the crown from the weather. It is important to have the arch of the hatch very strongly built, as it has to stand a lot of strain, and an iron support too near the fire soon corrodes and needs replacing. Another essential is that the site be as dry as possible and the foundation made solid with concrete; otherwise even a small kiln is liable to settle and crack. With a little extra expense a kiln of this kind could be banded round the impost and fireholes, thus considerably prolonging its life.

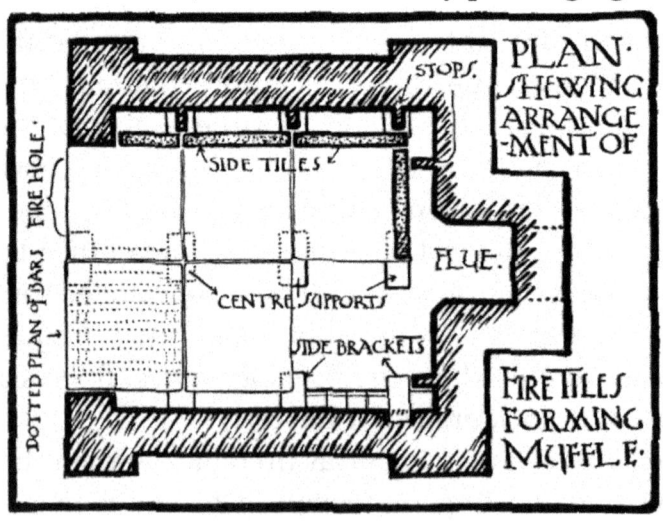

Fig. 72a

Fig. 72b

In firing this kiln about half a ton of coke and three quarters of a ton of good hard coal, giving a long flame, was used. Coke for the slow fire was first started on the bottom and maintained for sixteen or eighteen hours, lifted up on to the bars for another six or eight hours, when the saggars would begin to show signs of color.

The coal fire was then started about the 24th or 25th hour and continued another 18 hours, more or less, according to the varying conditions, making in all some 40 or 45 hours. This gave a very evenly graduated heat from cone 1 at the base to cone .03 at the top. Bags were tried experimentally, but whilst giving a more uniform heat, took much longer to fire up.

Basics of ... Pottery

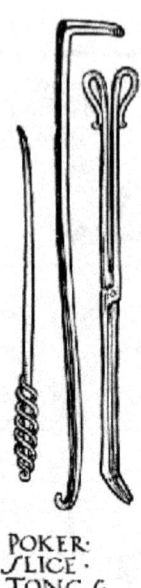

POKER·
SLICE·
TONGS·

Fig. 73

At the finish of the firing the fireholes were bricked up, the damper closed when the fires died down. In about 24 hours the vent and the hatch were eased a little at the top, and in 48 hours it was pulled down and the drawing commenced. Packed with the hard glazes at the bottom and the soft at the top this kiln answered excellently for the purposes for which it was required.

Fig. 74

Basics of ... Pottery

CHAPTER XVI
The Educational Value of Pottery

"The principal point in Education is that one's knowledge of the World begins at the right End."
                                        —Schopenhauer

The study of the fictile art of the potter, even from the theoretical side alone, cannot fail to quicken and broaden education. The antiquity of the craft, stimulating research amongst the records of ancient civilizations, brings to light customs and habits bearing very closely upon the earliest struggles of man to emancipate himself from mere brute surroundings. The primitive decorations rudely scratched on clay vessels antedate and forecast the hieroglyphic and sign languages of all nations.

It would be but hyperbole to claim that without clay the Mosaic tablets would have remained unwritten, but indubitably the clay cylinders of Assyria gave a strong impulse to the development of ciphering and writing and the spread of learning,—an impetus not to be derived from the obstinate granite medium so generally employed by the Egyptians.

It is this amenable ductile quality, so easily receptive of the most emotional touch, that has made and still makes clay such an admirable medium of expression for the young,—whether young in the history of the world or young in actual years. And this malleability is accompanied by a tenacity that permits slow building up, remodeling, and high finish, suitable to work of the most painstaking character. To this is added the fixed, unalterable quality imparted by fire, so that pottery more than any other craft preserves an imperishable record of the ages.

This positive chronicle is valuable alike to the savant or the student. Indeed the most trivial child's toys of the Hellenes, the quaint water pots of the Peruvian peasant, or the unassuming tea bowl of the esoteric followers of Riku may chance to convey to the sincere student a clearer idea of the habits and thoughts of their producers than many a pedantic treatise or translation.

> So lively shines
> In them Divine resemblance and such grace
> The hand that made them on their shape hath poured.
> —Milton

Coming down to points in close contact with the curricula of schools, we all subscribe to the dictum of Ruskin that "Everyone, from the King's son downwards, should learn to do something finely and thoroughly with his hands." What then more suitable than sympathetic clay wherein to fashion the first fancies of the child mind. It is a medium at once attractive and easy to mold, giving a tangibility and reality to forms and things that can never be obtained by drawing or painting. Then the limitless uses to which clay is put, and, with the development of hygiene, increasingly will be put, have the closest bearing upon the everyday life of the child. They are intimately connected with other studies that cannot fail to be rendered more attractive by working in clay.

But clay work is a branch now so universal that it seems unnecessary to dwell upon its advantages to the kindergartener.

The valuable remedial effects of clay work upon the defective are perhaps less widely known. The manipulation induces a most beneficial concentration and provides a fine discipline without a trace of inimical restraint. Turning to higher grades, the use of clays should foster an interest in the formation, composition, and disintegration of rocks, and in the properties of the products so engendered; in short, a liking for geology.

With the making of simple glazes and colors will awaken an intelligent curiosity concerning the nature of minerals and metals, their actions and reactions in the fire; a lively sympathy only awaiting a touch to turn it into a love for chemistry and physics. Then as power and ambition and craftsmanship develop, there must needs be a study of the history of ornament. This impinges too closely upon history and geography to fail to increase the student's attraction towards these more remote but allied fields.

Finally, is it not in the realm of æsthetics that there looms the ultimate reward? The proper pursuit of pottery must eventually lead us "towards that idealization of daily life ... and the road that connects the love of the beautiful with the love of the good is short and smooth" (President Eliot). In the hurried curricula of today art plays a rather sorry part. Little time indeed is left for contemplation, for the realization of all that beauty and harmony in our surroundings may mean to us in our everyday work.

The making of a bowl, with the concentration required to shape it in a manner at once beautiful and serviceable, must quicken the perception of beauty and sharpen the quality of judgment, not only for things fictile, but in far wider fields. Thus the things of everyday contact—the tableware, the chairs, the doors, the windows, pictures, ornaments, hangings, and fittings—will all come in for intelligent scrutiny and criticism. This in turn will be carried on and over into matters civic. This must result in a careful estimation, selection, and appreciation of our surroundings, bringing them into harmony with our cultivated thoughts and so enabling us to get through the day's work with the least amount of useless friction and with the greatest possible measure of enjoyment, well-being, and well-doing.

George J. Cox

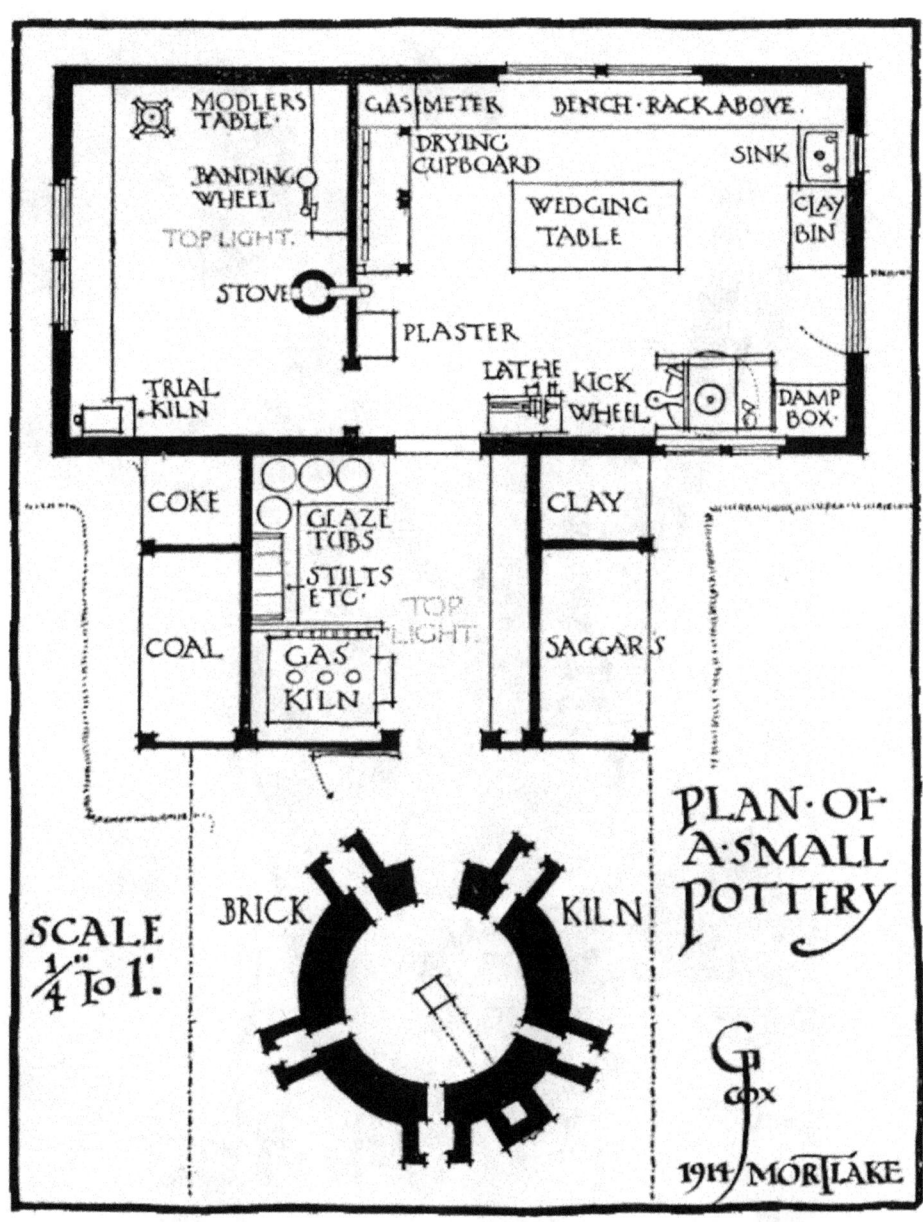

Basics of ... Pottery

APPENDIX I
The Equipment

The divinity that presides over potting is an expensive as well as an exacting mistress. The equipment of even a small pottery is, unfortunately, a matter of considerable expense. Try it from whatever angle we may there is the cost of the kiln to be faced, besides a host of other small but cumulative expenses. The first essential is, of course, a roomy workshop with if possible a top as well as a side light. If the craftsman means business, he should remember that the initial cost of a kiln is often in inverse ratio to its upkeep. If he would aspire to big things, full-bellied pots, plaques, reliefs, and figures,—and every craftsman would,—a brick kiln will be wanted. One holding a dozen saggars could be built, but where some experience has been obtained with materials and processes, a larger one would be more economical. With oil or gas kilns of the ordinary school size the cost of firing and the extra time is proportionately too great to permit of any but comparatively high-priced pots being turned out. This may serve in some cases, but usually it is not practical potting where a livelihood has to be obtained. Where only the painting is to be fired on, an oil or gas kiln is exactly what is wanted.

In this appendix is given a plan of a workshop that has all the equipment necessary for the whole-hearted pursuit of the craft. In such an one a good craftsman, capable of modeling and painting decently a figure or a panel, a good

Basics of ... Pottery

thrower, and a handy boy could work wonders. They would be capable of turning out a surprisingly wide range of "pots": jugs, mugs, pots, bottles, bowls, buttons, dishes, plaques, panels, vases, tiles, and statuettes,—useful and beautiful things. Anything in fact worth doing can be done except fine tableware or those articles that by their nature demand more mechanical accuracy than is possible, or even desirable, for a craftsman to exhibit. Where much plaster turning for molds was attempted, a lathe would be required; ordinarily the hiring of one should be practicable and expedient. Where only built or cast shapes were attempted, the wheel and its long years of drill might be dispensed with, and it is possible, with strong individual work of high finish and fine quality and the consequently restricted output, that an oil or gas kiln would give economically practicable results. Between the kiln for firing decoration simply painted on the ready-made shape to the full equipment here described will be found several modifications, but to try the craft without a kiln of some sort is an imbecile proceeding.

> Small brick kiln supplied with saggars.
> Small muffle kiln—oil or gas—for over-glaze and lusters.
> Small enameller's kiln for firing quick trials.
> Kick wheel, and tools for throwing.
> Clay bin, zinc-lined.
> Damp-box.
> Drying cupboard.
> Plaster bin.
> Pot boards and brackets.
> Table, strong and heavy.
> Clay: white, red, buff.

Plaster.
Glaze materials.
Oxides, lusters.
Under- and over-glaze colors.
Modeling tools, callipers.
Painter's outfit.
Brushes, straight-edges.
Shellac, beeswax, French chalk.
Gum arabic and tragacanth.
Glaze tubs, teak.
Sieves, glaze and slip, Nos. 80, 100, 120.
Buckets.
Bowls, enameled and earthenware.
Small porcelain ball mill, hand or power.
Spray and pump (respirator).
Small outfit for carpentry.
Files, sheet iron, and zinc, wire and cutters, cords, sandpaper.
Benches and shelves ad lib., odd cupboards, chairs, etc.,
Shovels and slicer for firing, tongs for trials.
Two large tubs and rubber tubing.
Sand and flint.
Spurs, props, fire tiles.
Tile boxes.
Disc (emery) for grinding.
Small pestle and mortar.
Jugs and funnel.
Potter's knife, sponges.
Whirler.
Turning tools and lathe.
Temperature indicators.

Basics of ... Pottery

Oil can, oil, waste.
Callipers and compass, rulers.

Most of this equipment has been previously described and needs no further comment.

The pot boards and brackets are simple but indispensable devices. The boards are about six feet long, iron shod or cross battened to prevent warping, and six or nine inches in width. The brackets of any serviceable kind are fixed to the wall at convenient distances. When throwing, turning, or glazing, the pots are stood on one of these boards to dry, and each board as filled is slipped onto the brackets. Thus the pots may be carried about to the kiln, drying cupboard, or glaze tubs without loss of time or frequent handling.

The table must be stout enough to withstand the heavy work of wedging and should have a top of hard wood. Teak or hard-wood glaze tubs have the advantage of not breaking either themselves or pots accidentally knocked against them. Further, some glazes stick badly to porcelain or enamel tubs.

Basics of ... Pottery

EQUIPMENT FOR A SMALL POTTERY

In the small pottery plotted here, the equipment and arrangement were as follows:

An anthracite stove with the pipe running into the large room warmed the workshop in winter, but no wet or half-dry pots were left where the frost could get at them.

The glaze materials, oxides, colors, painting paraphernalia, finished pots, trials, and trial kiln were in the small room. The wheel had a good top and side light.

The drying cupboard, plaster bin, and molds were at the end nearest the stove; the clay bin, damp-box, and sink farthest away.

All the walls were copiously supplied with brackets and shelves and handy benches.

Outside, in a well-built lean-to, was the muffle kiln for onglaze and luster decoration.

This was well bracketed and shelved for the biscuit, and here was done the glazing, handy for packing in the brick kiln just outside. This was protected from the weather and other lean-to's held the saggars, coke, and coal.

Basics of ... Pottery

EQUIPMENT FOR SCHOOLS

The teacher with ample funds and a free hand will find the previous chapter all-sufficient, but in many cases the purchase of a kiln will nearly exhaust the allowance and the rest of the equipment becomes sketchy.

The indispensable appliances are as follows:

A kiln, with fire tiles or shelves, props, spurs, and stilts, etc., for packing. A good clay bin and sieve for slip (No. 80) with a tub and two pails.

Scales and weights, pestle and mortar and glaze lawn (No. 100), shot for weights.

Plaster, for drying bats and working discs.

Large drip pan and three round pans.

Several jugs and bowls.

Spoons (wooden), knives, and big brushes.

Oil, gum, boards, strips, rolling pin.

Hammer, saw, iron straight-edge, sponges.

Glass slab and muller, palette knife and brushes for painting.

An atomizer or spray pump.

Glaze materials:

Kaolin, China stone, flint, silver sand, whiting, feldspar, borax. A supply of ground pitchers and grog, cones.

Metallic oxides:

Tin, white, oxide of, iron, copper, manganese, cobalt, etc.

Under-glaze colors to taste.

Glass jars with lids to contain materials. Gummed labels, India ink.

Basics of ... Pottery

For a school in the country or where ground is available, a kiln like the one shown at p. 164 should be practicable. It costs very little to build or to fire. Next comes the question of the clay. This is one of the most abundant of nature's materials, and almost any river bank or creek will supply clay of some kind. Any sort of clay near to hand should be thoroughly tested before going to other or distant sources.

The clay should be dried, then broken up with a hammer, and mixed with water, and the resultant "slurry" passed through a sieve (No. 80). The slip is allowed to settle and the water siphoned off. The thick slip is then dried on the plaster bats until stiff enough to work up between the hands. From this clay a tile, a plate, and a vase should be made and fired. If the pieces stand a fire of about 1100° (cone .03) without buckling, splitting, or crumbling, the clay should do quite well for school work. Possibly when screened fine enough for working, the clay may be too rich or *long* and will split at a moderate fire. Then the screenings might be pounded in the mortar, passed through the sieve, and added to the slip. Again, ground pitchers, fine grog, kaolin, or calcined flint could be tried as stiffening agents. In the unlikely event of the clay being too refractory or *short*, a portion of rich, fusible, or *fat* clay might be added, or the addition of powdered spar tested. (See chapter on Clays.) The color of the body will hardly matter for schools; indeed a brown, red, or cane-colored clay will give better results than a staring white paste, when working out simple school problems.

Where necessary, tin glaze could be used for a white ground, or an engobe; that is, a dip of white clay slip over the colored body. For glazing, a leadless glaze is strongly to be advised. Lead is often indispensable to the craftsman, and with care need not become a danger; but in schools a lead glaze is positively harmful.

A glaze with a borax base, if ground dry and mixed with water and re-ground before sieving, will give little trouble if used immediately. It will answer for all grade work and may be used for spraying, dipping, pouring, or painting, with absolute safety.

The ground pitchers and grog may be obtained by pounding up broken biscuit and pieces of fire tile, respectively. This, and the glaze grinding, is, of course, laborious work, and suggests correlation with the Physical Education Department. The drip pan and the round tins make excellent molds for casting drying bats and working bats.

For casting purposes plates and shallow bowls may be molded in one piece as described, p. 26. If no lathe be handy, glazed vases may be used as substitutes, the "waste" being added in plasticine to the neck and base.

For tile making, strips nailed on a stout board will serve in place of tile boxes. The clay is rolled out on cheesecloth with a rolling pin. Various other expedients for drying cupboards, damp-box, etc., will suggest themselves as the course develops.

The above equipment need not be very costly. With it the students should be capable of producing all kinds of tiles, built, pressed, and cast shapes, decorated in relief, with inlays or in colors or glaze.

Basics of ... Pottery

APPENDIX II
Glossary

Alumina, or Oxide of Aluminium, is one of the most abundant of earths. Combined with silica it is the chief constituent of kaolins and China clays. It imparts refractory qualities to clays and is an indispensable ingredient of pure glazes. Pure alumina or calcined Aluminium is a chemical product.

Ammonia.—A volatile gaseous matter, found in some clays. Alkaline in action.

Antimony.—A silver-white metallic element, used with other oxides as a colorant or to give opacity in glazes.

Arsenic.—A non-metallic volatile element, used in glaze making.

Barytes.—A heavy spar used with clays to introduce density and vitrescence.

Bauxite.—A very aluminous earth, used in preparation of pure alumina and to render clays refractory.

Boracic Acid.—The natural and, usually, impure product (boric acid being free from chemicals).

Borax.—The combined chemical product of soda and boracic acid. Used as a strong flux in glazes.

Calcined Bones.—The residuum of burned bones, used to stiffen artificial porcelain.

Calcined Kaolin.—Kaolin after it has been subjected to heat to drive off the water combined with it.

Calcium Carbonate (Whiting).—Found as a white rock, and ground to pure powder. Used with clays for soft bodies. Gives durability to glazes.

Calcium Oxide (Lime).—A widely distributed earthy matter. Imparts fusibility to clays, in nearly all of which it is present in varying proportions.

Chrome, Oxide of.—Used in making greens, browns, and blacks. Stands a high fire.

Basics of ... Pottery

Clays

Ball Clay.—Blue and black. Very plastic clays. Used with non-plastic materials, such as flint, stone, feldspar, or whiting, to form fine earthenwares.

Cane and Red Clays.—Clays colored by the presence of ferric oxide, and used extensively for bricks, terra-cotta tiles, and common pottery.

China Clay.—A yellowish-white, non-vitreous clay, product of the decomposition of granitic or felspathic rocks. Cornish China clay is exceptionally white, pure, and plastic. It is widely used with China, or Cornwall stone and calcined bones, to make bone porcelain. Feldspar is added to render it vitreous. Mixed with ball clays, pipe clays, flint, and stone, it makes the various classes of earthen and stone wares.

Pipe Clay.—A very white, smooth clay. Less plastic than ball clays. Much used for making slips, engobes, and enamels.

Saggar Clays or Fire Clays.—Coarse refractory clays strengthened by the addition of grog, used for saggars, fire tiles, and bricks.

Cobalt Oxide.—The oxide of the steel-grey hard metal. Extremely valuable in pottery, making all shades of blue for under-glaze printing or staining. With iron or copper gives blue-greens.

Copper, Oxides of, and Carbonate.—Red, green, and black oxides of copper have been of the utmost value to potters. They are used to produce green, blue, turquoise, red, and crimson. Its extraordinary changes in reducing or oxidizing fires are of the greatest interest to the experimenter.

Cornish or China Stone.—A rock composed of feldspar and quartz. Its vitrification (about 1400° C.) imparts hardness and density to China clays. It is a valuable constituent of glazes. First known as "moorstone" or "growan."

Earthy Colorants.—Rarely used in modern commercial pottery, except for salt-glazed jars, crocks, and peasant pottery.

Feldspar.—A fusible rock found almost pure or in combination with potash and soda, the greater the percentage of alkalis the more fusible being the spar. It is used to replace more refractory materials in clay and to stiffen glazes.

Flint.—A pure silica with slight traces of calcium. Found in pebble form on seashores. Calcined and ground to a white powder, it is widely used to impart whiteness and strength to clays. Invaluable for bedding and packing in kilns. Used with the fluxes,—lead, borax, potash, and soda,—to make glazes and glass.

Fluorspar.—A combination of fluorine and calcium, more fusible than feldspar, and of a white color, feldspar being pink.

Galena.—Lead sulfide, a highly poisonous material used on "peasant" pottery, giving a soft, yellowish, transparent glaze.

Gold.—Used in solution for delicate purples and lusters.

Gypsum.—When calcined gypsum becomes plaster of Paris, these two materials, together with the allied marble, limestone, and alabaster, are widely used in pastes (such as

Parian), slips, engobes, and variously to impart fusibility or color properties to glazes.

Iron, Oxides of.—Have a wide range of color, from yellow to purple. They are used to stain glazes and color bodies. They impart fusibility to clays and are carefully excluded from fine white bodies.

Kaolin.—A fine, white, very pure, and infusible China clay, almost pure alumina and silica. Chiefly used in the manufacture of porcelain and fine earthenware.

Lead (Oxides and Carbonates of). White Lead, Red Lead, Litharge.—Are very widely used as a safe and cheap flux. Poisonous. It cannot be used in those glazes that have to stand a high fire.

Lime. (*See* **Calcium.**)

Lynn Sand. (*See* **Quartz Sand.**)

Magnesia.—A white metallic element present in small quantities in most clays.

Manganese.—The black and brown oxides of this hard metal are much used to stain slips and bodies, and to color glazes brown or purple.

Marls.—Amorphous deposits of lime, sand, and clay, very coarse in texture. Used in making saggars, drain pipes, and similar appliances.

Nickel.—A hard metallic element, the oxides of which are found useful in preparing blacks, greys, and greens.

Niter or Potassium Nitrate, or Saltpeter.—A vitreous and aqueous compound, used in some glazes.

Plaster of Paris. (*See* **Gypsum.**)

Potash.—Potassium carbonate or the leached ashes of plants. Used from earliest times as a powerful alkaline flux.

Potash, Bichromate of.—Used for pinks and

crystalline effects. Poisonous.

Quartz or Quartz Sand.—Like Lynn or silver sand. This mineral is pure silica and free from lime, although the sands may contain some small percentage of iron. Used much like flint for bedding or with alkaline fluxes for the finest glazes.

Rutile. Oxide of Titanium.—Used variously to impart a yellow tinge to porcelain, and color and irregularity to some glazes.

Salt.—Sodium chloride. Sometimes used in glazes, but best known in connection with salt glazing. It vaporizes at about 1200° C., forming a silicate or hard, thin skin of glaze over the clay.

Silica.—A hard, colorless crystalline element; found pure, as in quartz, or in combination with alumina and alkalis, as in all clays. Present in all glazes.

Soda. Sodium Carbonate.—Product of the decomposition of salts with acids. It is a strong alkaline flux and much used in glaze and glass-making.

Silver Sand. (*See* **Quartz**.)

Tin, Oxide of.—Used from the earliest times to impart opacity to glazes.

Tincal. (*See* **Borax**.)

Titanium. (*See* **Rutile**.)

Whitening. (*See* **Lime**.)

Zinc, Oxide of.—A white metallic oxide; used to brighten and stabilize glazes and colors.

POTTER'S TERMS

Bags.—Chimneys or walls of fire bricks built to protect the ware from flame.

Baitings.—The feed of fuel during firing.

Bat.—Any flat slab of plaster, biscuit, or fire clay.

Biscuit.—The fired but unglazed clay.

Blowing.—The shattering of the clay shape when biscuiting. Usually due to hurried firing or the sudden access of heat, and the consequent generation of steam.

Blunger.—A machine for mixing clay.

Bungs.—Piles of filled saggars.

Chuck or Chum.—The cone or cap used to support shapes during turning on the lathe.

Clamming.—The wet marl, sand, or siftings applied to cracks in the hatches or doors of kilns to retain the heat during firing.

Craze.—The minute cracks that appear in a badly fitting glaze. When arrived at by design, as in some Chinese work, it is termed a crackle, but there is then no fissure.

Drawing.—Unpacking the kiln after firing.

Engobe.—A dip or outer covering of slip; usually applied to inferior bodies to improve their appearance.

Fat.—Clays that are sticky or greasy are sometimes termed fat by potters.

Fettle.—To touch up, and remove traces of seams, cast lines, etc.

Fluxes.—Those materials which by their addition to paste or glaze render them fusible, although they may not always be fusible themselves.

Glost.—The glazed ware, usually applied to the glaze in firing, as glost-oven.

Green.—The clay shapes before biscuiting.

Jigger.—The wheel on which shapes are molded with the aid of a jolley or profile.

Joggle.—The natch or key in a mold to insure correct adjustment and prevent slipping.

Lawn.—The fine mesh gauze through which glazes are strained.

Long.—A clay is termed long if very ductile and tenacious.

Muffle.—Usually the fire-clay box or interior of a small kiln, but applied to any kiln to the inside of which the flames have no access.

Natch. (*See* **Joggle.**)

Oxidizing.—The ordinary method of firing gives an atmosphere in which there is always sufficient oxygen to consume all the carbon or combustible gases. If oxygen is present in excess, it causes reactions known as oxidizing.

Pitchers.—Finely ground biscuit. Added to some clays to increase refractories or porosity. Molds made in such clays and fired are termed pitcher molds.

Potsherds.—Any broken biscuit or pot, sometimes used for pitchers.

Potting.—A colloquialism used to designate the ceramic industry.

Pugging.—The roll of infusible clay placed between each saggar when building bungs.

Reducing.—The reaction that accompanies the introduction of smoke or gas containing carbon in a very finely divided state into a kiln during the process of firing glaze. Reduction is now widely employed in obtaining fine effects.

Refractory.—Hard, infusible.

Rich.—Used of clays that are long and fusible, such as red clays.

Riffle.—A grooved and toothed plaster tool of steel.

Saggars.—Or seggers. The fire-clay receptacles in which the glazed ware is set during the firing.

Setters.—Supports used when packing friable biscuit.

Short.—A word used to denote a clay that crumbles or is difficult to pull up on the wheel.

Sieve.—Sometimes called a lawn, more correctly a

screen for clay or slip.

Slip.—The sieved clay or paste in creamy liquid condition as used for slip decoration, engobes, or casting.

Slub or Slurry.—Clay mixed with water but not sieved, as with slip.

Spy.—The small hole, kept plugged, through which tests and cones are observed.

Stunt.—Or dunt. To crack or split on cooling.

Turning.—The shaving down of the clay shape on a lathe, to impart lightness and finish.

U. G.—Under-glaze (applied to colors).

Vent.—A hole to aid the even distribution of fire in a kiln or to accelerate the cooling off.

Waster.—Commercially, a spoiled pot; defective ones are termed "seconds."

Wedging.—The beating or slamming operation usually employed to expel air or correct inequalities just before clay is used by the thrower.

Whirler.—A circular support pivoting on its center, used in casting or banding; similar to a banding wheel, but usually heavier.

MATERIALS, TERMS, ETC.

C = Combining Weight
E = Equivalent Weight

	Symbol
Alumina (calcined)	Al_2O_3
Alumina (hydrated)	$Al_2O_3 \cdot 3H_2O$
Aluminium	Al
Ammonia	NH_3
Antimony	Sb
Antimony oxide	SbO
Arsenic	As
Barium (metallic element)	Ba
Barium carbonate	$BaCO_3$
Barytes	$BaSO_4$
Bauxite	
Bismuth	Bi
Borax (crystals)	$Na_2B_4O_7 \cdot 10H_2O$
Boric acid (crystals)	$B_2O_3 \cdot 3H_2O$
Boric acid (dry)	B_2O_3
Boron (metallic element)	B
Calcined bones	
Calcined kaolin	
China clay (fine)	$Al_2O_3 \cdot 2SiO_2$
Calcium oxide (lime)	CaO
Calcium carbonate	$CaCO_3$
China stone	
Cornish stone	$8SiO_2 \cdot 2Al_2O_3 \cdot K_2O$

189

Basics of ... Pottery

Chrome oxide	Cr_2O_3
Chromium	Ca
Cobalt	Co
Cobalt oxide	Co_2O_3
Cobalt oxide (black)	Co_2O_4
Copper	Cu
Copper oxide (black)	CuO
Earthy colorants	
Ochres	
Siennas	
Umbers	
Feldspar	$6SiO_2 \cdot Al_2O_3 \cdot K_2O$
Flint (calcined)	SiO_2
Fluorspar	CaF_2
Galena (lead sulfide)	PbS
Gold	Au
Gypsum (plaster of Paris, if calcined)	$CaSO_4 \cdot 2H_2O$
Iron	Fe
Iron oxide	Fe_2O_3
Iridium	Ir
Kaolin (see calcined kaolin)	$Al_2O_3 \cdot 2SiO_2 \cdot 2H_2O$
Lead (metal)	Pb
Lead carbonate	$PbCO_2$
Lead, red oxide of	Pb_3CO_4
Lime (see calcium oxide or carbonate)	CaO
Lynn sand (see silver sand)	SiO_2
Magnesia (calcined)	MgO
Magnesia (carbonate)	$MgO \cdot CO_2$
Manganese, carbonate	$MnCO_3$
Manganese (metal)	Mn
Manganese oxide (or black)	MnO_2
Nickel (metal)	Ni
Nickel oxide	NiO

Niter	KNO_3
Pearl ash or potash	KOH
Plaster of Paris (calcined gypsum)	$CaSO_4 \cdot \tfrac{1}{2}H_2O$
Platinum	Pt
Potash, bichromate of	$K_2Cr_2O_7$
Potassium carbonate	K_2CO_3
Potassium oxide	K_2O
Quartz	SiO_2
Quartz sand	
Rutile (see titanium)	
Salt	$NaCl$
Silica	SiO_2
Silver sand (or quartz sand)	SiO_2
Silver (metal)	Ag
Soda ash (calcined)	Na_2CO_3
Soda crystals	$Na_2CO_3 \cdot 10\,H_2O$
Sodium oxide	Na_2O
Tincal (see borax)	
Tin (metal)	Sn
Tin oxide (white)	SnO_2
Titanium oxide (rutile)	TiO_2
Uranium (metal)	U
Uranium, oxide of	U_3O_8
Whitening (see lime carbonate)	
Zinc (metal)	Zn
Zinc oxide (white)	ZnO

Meet the Author

George J. Cox garnered acclaim as a pottery instructor at the Teachers College of Columbia University. Vases by Cox are quite collectible. He is noted for his Mortlake art pottery, large ornamental wares inspired by early Chinese styles and decorated with monochrome glazes. His Mortlake Pottery workshop in London closed down when he moved to the US to teach.

AbsolutelyAmazingeBooks.com
or AA-eBooks.com